BRAVE ENOUGH
TO CHANGE

by

MICHAEL CALAM

Brave Enough to Change
By Michael Calam
2024

Published by Michael Calam
www.michaelcalam.com

Copyright © Michael Calam
ISBN 978-0-646-89172-9

Printed in Australia by Ingram Spark Pty Ltd

"They say a person needs just three things to be truly happy in this world: someone to love, something to do, and something to hope for."

Tom Bodett

Dedicated to my wife Sandra, this story is as much hers as it is mine. Without her beside me I don't know if I would be here to tell this story today.

To Chris and Kasey, your partners Sarah and Mike and especially to Azzy, Kai, Hamish, Nellie and Billy. I couldn't love you all any more than I do.

For Rachael, who inspired and encouraged me to finally tell my story. I hope that one day others get to hear your story and become as inspired by you as I am.

Contents

Introduction..1

PART I – Resilience: We're Tougher Than We Think.........**8**

Chapter 1 – Rock Bottom..11

Chapter 2 – It Started With….....................................25

Chapter 3 – Fear Factor...31

Chapter 4 – The Moments That Test Us.....................39

Chapter 5 – One Bad Decision Can Cost You Everything....45

Chapter 6 – The Final Straw......................................55

Chapter 7 – Finding Resilience..................................63

PART II – Owning Change...................................**72**

Chapter 8 – What Happened Next?...........................75

Chapter 9 – Family Secrets.......................................85

Chapter 10 – How Do I Learn?..................................95

Chapter 11 – The Lesson...99

Chapter 12 – Choice and Change......................................103

Chapter 13 – Courage...109

Chapter 14 – Uncomfortable Conversations....................115

Chapter 15 – Commitment..119

Chapter 16 – Change and Growth......................................127

Chapter 17 – Owning Change...133

PART III – We Get to Choose Our Mindset..............**138**

Chapter 18 – In An Instant..141

Chapter 19 – Full Moon...147

Chapter 20 – Make Every Moment Count......................153

Chapter 21 – My Theory of Relativity...............................161

Chapter 22 – My Choice...163

Introduction

I WANT TO TALK ABOUT change. I think that most of us don't think or talk enough about it.

We're born to change. We grow up and then we grow old. Change is written into our very DNA. It's not just our bodies that change over time, our memory, emotions and behaviours also change as well.

We change as we learn and grow. We adapt and I hope, over time we grow wiser.

It's not just internally. Change happens everywhere. The world changes around us as we change the world.

I've spent most of my life reacting. Responding to events and to my environment. Dealing with the outcomes from the shit decisions I've made, shit that other people did to me and the random shit that life has thrown at me. Change has been constant.

The moment that I stopped reacting was the moment that changed my life. When I realised that I could take control and decide who I wanted to be, not who others thought that I should be. Because trying to be something other than who I am almost killed me in the past.

I'm going to tell my story and what I've learned after years of being tossed around by life events. How I've stopped reacting and taken the front seat in directing my life. Making conscious change to live the life that I want to live.

I've been knocked down. I've hit rock bottom and I've made my way back up again. I'll probably get knocked down again. Life sometimes does that. There are two lessons I want to share from my own experiences. The first is that we can get back up again. The second is how to do it. I think that they are probably the two most profound life lessons that any of us can learn.

I'm sharing my story because I hope that I can inspire and help others to improve their lives. Whatever you're facing, whether it's work, relationships or just life, I hope that hearing about someone else's journey can help you to find your pathway. How you too can take control of your life, even when life throws unexpected challenges at you.

My story has been broken into three parts. The first part will be to tell you my story leading up to my attempted suicide and why that seemed to be an option for me. I'll be open with you about why I went down this path and what stopped me and allowed me to be here today. In that section I'll talk about the weeks, months and years leading up to that point and what I felt along the way. Once I've told you that part of my story I'll then discuss what I have learned from that experience and the benefit of twenty plus years of self-reflection to help me better understand human resilience.

Telling this will frame where I am today and what I learned from hitting that point.

The second part of my story discusses the period of my life post that decision and what I learned through being forced to change. There I'll discuss what I came to understand about taking control of change in my life and how I started to make conscious choices to help me to become who I am today.

The third and final part of this book is titled We Get to Choose our Mindset. There are some personal stories I will share with you that have helped me to build a mindset of gratitude and happiness.

Along the way I'm going to talk about choices. My message to you is that no matter how rough it gets and how trapped we may feel, that we always have choices.

I'm grateful to be here, there have been times when I thought that I wouldn't make it. I guess that we probably all have those near misses. Those times when things have gone sideways, and we've seen our lives flash before our eyes. Then there were the times where I thought that I couldn't make it.

I was a cop and I had lots of those exciting adventures. The thrill of the chase, the pub brawls, the moment of truth when you're up against someone who is trying their best to physically hurt or kill you. The truth is that we all knew about those aspects when we signed up for the job, we went into that side with our eyes wide open and if I'm to be honest, with an anticipation that we would get to experience those moments. This book is not about the physical danger, it's about the stories that broke my heart, that scarred my soul and made me struggle to carry on.

Many people who know me today don't know my past. They see my happiness, my cheerfulness and my optimism and I guess they probably believe that is who I've always been. I want to talk about how I arrived at that point after walking through the dark days.

Don't get me wrong, it's not always rosy in my world. Regardless of how much I've learned, shit still happens. I'm like everyone else. I have my moments when I'm down, when the way forward is hard.

The thing is that I've learned to work my way through those times. Most of all I've also learned to let others help me to work my way through those times. I've found my people. The people who know when I need to get a laugh, but also the people who know when to just listen or to just be there beside me.

Learning to let others help me was probably the most difficult lesson for me. And most importantly it's been about learning who those others are. I wasn't always willing to let others help me. Over the coming pages I will talk about how I tried to face things on my own. How I pushed people away from me when I probably needed them the most.

We can tell ourselves that we're too proud to accept help. I did that. That's bullshit. I realised later in life that the reason I didn't accept help when I needed it most was because I was too scared. Here's one of the corporate buzzwords coming, vulnerability. Truth is there's no better word for it. To ask for or to accept helps means that we must be vulnerable and show our weaknesses, and that can be bloody frightening. To be vulnerable means that we must give people the ability to hurt us. There's a quote about love in this context from E. Lockhart that means a lot to me:

> *"Love is when you give someone else the power to destroy you, and you trust them not to do it."*

I was too afraid to give others that power over me. This is the story of how I found my way. I don't know what you've faced or what you will face in the future. I can only tell you my story and hope that it helps you.

In telling some of the stories of my past I'm going to speak about some sensitive subjects, and I make no apologies for that because it's my story. Fair warning, if you find the topics of suicide, rape, or child abuse too hard to deal with, then please find another book to read. I don't blame you. They're not topics I would have chosen for myself, but we don't always get to choose the plots of our own storylines.

During the process of writing this I've been asked why I would want to share such personal stories. Some shit happened to me because people kept secrets. I'm telling my story so that maybe others can learn how bad it can be to keep those kinds of secrets.

I'm telling my story because there is shit that I went through that I know others go through but like me, might be too afraid to admit it. I want you to know that you're not alone. That there are people out there who care, even strangers – like me, who care about you.

I'm telling my story because maybe there is shit that you need to face. Tough decisions that you will need to make in your life that may hurt you or hurt others. Choices that will terrify you about your job, your business, your relationships, or your life. I want to share my struggles so that you can hopefully find the strength to do the things that you either need or want to do.

This is my playbook, and I'm writing it with all the rawness of my fears and failures. It's the story of how I learned to deal with trauma. It's about how I've personally learned to cope with hitting rock bottom and to find a way to build a life I'm happy with after that. It's not the story of someone who went on to win an Olympic medal, build a business empire or become a celebrity. It's the story of a guy who has learned how to find courage and to face change in his ordinary life. It's how I became brave enough to change.

Throughout the following pages I'll talk about some of the incidents I faced as a cop and in those I have changed the names of the people involved. For those of you who shared these experiences with me this is through no lack of respect, rather it's to respect that you can choose your own time and place to tell your story, if at all.

For those of you who do read on, thank you for listening. I hope that you can take something from my experiences that will help you in your life.

PART 1

Resilience: We're Tougher Than We Think

I'm tougher than I thought I was.
Even when I thought that I couldn't
make it, I somehow did.

CHAPTER 1

Rock Bottom

"Rock bottom became the solid foundation on which I rebuilt my life."

J.K. Rowling

I'M GOING TO START by talking about hitting rock bottom. It's hard for me to write about this. I'm not proud of letting myself get to this point. If I'm going to talk about my journey at all then this is a pivotal moment for me. It's not pretty but if I'm going to talk about the lessons that I learned from that then you need to hear the raw truth.

I was once a cop and while I was there, I hit my breaking point. Literally suicidal.

I tried to keep on going. I tried to put on a brave face. That's what we're taught as boys. Men don't cry, men don't whinge. As a cop you definitely don't admit that you're struggling, you would become an outcast. In my mind I had to be the person that others expected me to be. To be strong, stoic and resilient.

Later, I'll describe the culture of the Queensland Police Service in the 90's but let's just say that while the organisation was trying to change for the better, on the ground weakness or fear was not tolerated.

There was a mantra I had lived by. One which I repeated to myself over and over when things got tough.

Failure is not an option.

Underneath it all, I knew that I wasn't succeeding. I knew that I had to make a change but I couldn't see any other options and I was too afraid to admit that I wasn't coping. I couldn't bear to see myself fail.

For a start, I'd reached a point where I couldn't sleep.

I tried to fix that with alcohol. If I could get drunk enough, then I would pass out. And trust me, that seemed attractive. Have you ever just wanted to go to sleep and let your mind switch off from all your problems?

That's all I wanted. To go to sleep and forget about everything.

The problem was that I just could not get to sleep. I'd lay there staring at the ceiling with my thoughts racing and circling. No solutions, just what ifs, guilt, and problems.

I'd drink. Not the fun, at the pub with mates kind of drinking. The go home and eat a couple of bottles of wine on your own kind of drinking. However, it was never enough to keep me asleep. That's the problem with booze, it can be great at helping you to doze off or even to pass out. But then a few hours later I'd be awake again.

After midnight. Shit, I hated that time. They call it the witching hour. Definitions vary but it's for me it's always been somewhere between midnight and 4am. The time that folklore tells us that supernatural events occur. I've read that it's to do with our circadian rhythm, that this is the time when we're at our most vulnerable to those intrusive thoughts. Other books I've read tell me this is where our primal fears reside from our days of living in caves and when the nocturnal predators lurk. There's irony for me in that view.

For me it would be the time that I would wake up terrified, my heart hammering in my chest. Nightmares and memories would merge together so that I couldn't tell what was real and what was imagination.

The memories were horrible enough. I'm going to talk about them later in this book.

But when the nightmares kicked in then that's when the terror would come. I've seen some horrible stuff in my life, but our imaginations can always take it to the next level.

I guess that most people grow out of a fear of the dark, well at least I hope that they do. Do you remember as a kid being scared to look at the shadows in your bedroom but also feeling compelled to do so? When your imagination tells you that there's something there, but you don't want it to sneak up on you, so you stare into the darkness anyway.

I've heard people talking about not wanting to have their foot hanging over the edge of the bed in case something touches it in the night, knowing that it will never happen but still tucking it under the sheets, nonetheless. What if your nightmares were so real that you'd wake up convinced that someone or something was there?

I wasn't afraid of being alone in the dark. I was afraid of not being alone in the dark. Does that make sense?

For me it wasn't just the memories of my work as a cop that haunted me. Underneath them was an older, deeper trauma from childhood. I'd never outgrown those childhood fears of the dark because for me the monster had been so goddam real. I knew that the predators came out in the dark and would come for small children in their beds.

In that terrible time after midnight, I would once again be a four-year-old boy waiting for my grandfather Bill to come into my room and rape me again.

I'd escaped those nightmares and memories for years but the build up of trauma as a cop brought it all back and blended them in with the horrors I'd experienced in the job.

Whenever they came, I was always terrified. Powerless and completely vulnerable.

But it wasn't just at night. I had reached a point where wherever I went, I would always sit with my back to the wall.

That's a habit that I've never gotten rid of. I've since learned that it's not uncommon for cops, soldiers, and trauma victims to do the same. It's part of the hypervigilance that comes with trauma. We sit with our backs to the wall, and we'll generally be aware of every person in the room and where the exits are. You regularly tap your belongings in your pockets, wallet, keys, phone from the habit of regularly checking your work kit, gun, handcuffs, ammo. It's a heightened sense of situational awareness. Fortunately for me it's more of a habit now than what it was then.

The term "triggered" is used a lot today to describe things that evoke a strong reaction. For me at that time in my life, my mind created triggers out of the most mundane of situations. That sudden panic and flood of heart hammering adrenaline and then afterwards the weakness and confusion of trying to understand the wash of emotions. It was fucking exhausting.

I was always on high alert and so, so quick to anger.

Of course, I now know that all these issues were from post-traumatic stress disorder (PTSD). I'd reached a point where it had me deep in its grip and even in the bright light of day I could never relax. I was constantly on edge. Subconsciously I was always reliving every battle. Small things would trigger bursts of adrenaline and then leave me weak with exhaustion afterwards.

Most people understand the fight or flight reaction, where when we're threatened our bodies explode with a physiological response enabling us to be ready to either defend ourselves or run away. A good friend and mentor of mine, Steve Sharp, has since taught me that the primal areas of our brains can't distinguish a difference between a psychological threat and a physical one. Mine certainly couldn't.

PTSD stole a lot from me. At that time in my life, I should have been a young guy building out the possibilities of a full life. Instead, I was struggling to tie my shoes up in the mornings. I wanted to leave "the job" but I simply couldn't see a way out. I was more terrified of making that change than I was of staying in a job that was killing me.

I'd been a cop since I was eighteen. It had happened by accident.

School had been very easy for me. Academically that is, not socially. I coasted through every subject with minimal effort. Sounds like a brag but unfortunately, it's not. I picked up things easily, but I was a lazy student. I never did any homework or assignments because there was no-one at home who had any interest in checking in on me. I read a lot and I think that helped. Maths, physics, chemistry, and graphics were subjects that somehow just made sense to me and so I coasted, did well in the exams and let those grades carry me through. I'd thought about going on to university to study architecture but in our family, there was no drive for that. Instead, there was an imperative to go out and earn.

After finishing year twelve Ron, my stepdad got me a job working in the abattoir where he'd worked for the past couple of decades. I hated the work, but I made decent money, so I did that for a while.

I remember my "oh shit" moment. I was younger and fitter than Ron and so finally a week came where I'd put in a lot of overtime and managed to earn more than him for the week. Suddenly I saw him in a new light. At that stage he was in his forties but prematurely old. His hands and arms scarred from slipped knives. The creaks and groans of his bad back and his habitual scowl. I had a vision of my life twenty years from then and I wanted it to be anything other than that.

Coincidentally the Queensland Police Service was running a recruiting campaign at that time. A couple of years prior the old Queensland Police Force had been renamed and revamped following recommendations from the Fitzgerald Inquiry into police corruption. The government was making a push to create a more professional policing group and so they were looking for new recruits who either had existing tertiary education or other professional qualifications. As part of this blanket uplift in their standards they were advertising that they would put new recruits through a new university-based training program in their academy year which would equate to the first year of a degree.

To me, it ticked all the boxes. I could start my university education while being paid to do so. In my naïve seventeen-year-old mind I saw myself pursuing a career as a police psychologist, maybe even a criminal profiler. Too many novels and not enough careers counselling or mentoring influenced my decision-making process.

After passing all of the entry requirements I was accepted into an intake of one hundred and twenty recruits. I moved into the academy at Oxley.

Within two weeks I was hooked. For the first time in my life, I felt like I belonged somewhere. Living in at the academy and getting pushed physically and mentally was what I had needed.

Esprit de corps. I felt it in my bones.

We were young, we were fit, and the academy put us through hell to make us come together and realise our limits. I loved it. I hadn't sought it out as a career, but I found it calling to me.

There was another element that I had never realised. All my life I had been at the mercy of bullies. I was a skinny, awkward kid who had moved through about sixteen different primary schools and so had never built a network of friends and support-ers. I'd had Bill in my life along with two older stepbrothers who hadn't made my childhood that easy.

I hated bullies with a passion. I hated those who prey on the weak. I'd just never thought that I could do anything about it. Suddenly I realised that I could. The academy and the QPS gave me the tools and the capability to stand up for the oppressed. I know that sounds kind of wanky but for me it was so true. I felt a real calling to help those who needed protecting and after a lifetime of being powerless I finally received the training and encouragement to stand up for others. To stand up for myself.

Which is why it hurt so much to realise that the other parts of the job were killing me.

I could have caught bad guys for the rest of my life, but the death and the trauma ruined me. I hadn't built the resilience to overcome the things that I would see.

Policing is one of those jobs that becomes an identity, espe-cially when you spend time working in small communities. It had become part of who I was. Again the esprit de corps, only in a different way. We were a tribe apart in the community. There was an ingrained "them and us" mentality that was re-enforced in every part of our culture.

I found it very difficult to imagine doing anything else.

Reaching out to careers advisers and recruiters didn't help me at all. Most of them couldn't see any transferrable skills and so their only suggestions were to look at jobs in the security industry. There's nothing wrong with that, but in my mind if I was going to work in that space I may as well stay a cop. It was the same type of work, with less of the power to make a difference.

I felt trapped. Deep down I knew that I'd reached the point where I couldn't go on, but I could see no other choices. Have you ever reached a point where you can't remember the last time that you laughed?

That was where I was at.

I don't think that I did myself any favours in that regard. Because through all of this I kept my mask firmly in place. I couldn't let anyone know how broken I was, how weak.

I was so afraid.

When Robyn Williams committed suicide, the world was shocked. I wasn't. I completely got it. He was always the funniest man in the room, and I could relate to that because I've always been the class clown. The more I read about Robyn Williams the more I identified with him. He could make the room howl with laughter while inside I guess he was crying silent tears.

I would never let the people around me see the despair that I was feeling. I don't think I could even really articulate what I was feeling but it just felt that there was simply no future for me. I pushed everyone who cared about me away. I walked out of the relationship with my girlfriend Sandra, who is now my wife. God, I put her through hell during that time. I pushed her away and wanted her to hate me. I didn't want anyone to care about me if I took my life.

I gave up.

Every day was such a hard slog. Putting my boots on for work would reduce me to tears and I would just sit there on the edge of the bed crying, unable to tie my own shoelaces. Only when I was alone though. Sandra saw me crying and she always tried to help but I was in such a dark place that I kept pushing her away.

I would turn up to work and put up a brave face. It was really, really hard.

I'd started taking my revolver home from work. We weren't supposed to however nobody ever checked on that. When I'd worked up in Cairns and the far north of Queensland many of us had regularly taken our guns home. Sometimes some of us would catch up on farms and do some shooting practice and when I'd worked out in Cape York, we'd often take our revolvers with us if we went out hunting roos or pigs. But this was different, I was at the point where I wanted my gun with me if it got too much for me.

I've been to the scenes of many suicides over the years. I've seen every screwed-up way that people have taken or tried to take their own lives. The failures had been horrifying. People who had tried and failed and simply permanently disabled themselves. I didn't want that.

I'd also seen the torment that loved ones have felt when they found these poor broken souls in whatever hellish situation, they'd used to end it. I didn't want to inflict that on anybody.

I didn't want anybody I knew to see me like that. I came up with a plan for my suicide.

It was a simple plan. I hired a car and booked a room out in a bed and breakfast in a town called Stanthorpe. Stanthorpe is a beautiful area about three hours drive from Brisbane and it's very popular for its wineries and farm stays.

The area appealed to me because I didn't know any of the cops out around Stanthorpe and there were plenty of beautiful, isolated country spots where I could enact my plan without interruption.

Saving money wasn't high on my agenda at that point so for the drive out there I hired a convertible. One last extravagance.

I drove for hours with the top down and the wind in my face. There's a song I listened to over and over on repeat. I do that at the best of times, I find it soothing.

This music is an instrumental by Moby, called Everloving. It's music that always makes me think of the end of a movie or a sad story. I played that song over and over and it felt like it was the final track in the soundtrack of my life.

I cried almost non-stop during that entire drive.

When I arrived in Stanthorpe it was dark. I drove to the bottleshop, and I picked up a couple of bottles of wine. Ironic that I went to a bottle shop in the middle of about thirty local wineries, right?

After I checked in to my room I sat quietly in there and drank both bottles of wine. Then I got into bed, and I suppose that I passed out. Again ironically, for the first time in what felt like years I slept through the night.

My alarm went off just before sunrise.

I packed up my things, tidied the room and left in the darkness.

In the cold before dawn, I randomly drove down roads, always choosing those that narrowed until I found a place that felt isolated enough for me to watch the sun rise one more time.

I really wanted to see that one last sunrise and I didn't want to die in the dark.

It's hard to describe how calm I felt then, how peaceful.

Most people don't get suicide. It's a very selfish act. I understand that. Many years earlier I had turned my back on religion, God, and any belief in an afterlife. I believed and still do that when it ends, we face oblivion.

And oh man, that's what I wanted more than anything. The thought of not thinking, not feeling, not being was so fucking irresistible. To not hurt, to not be afraid anymore. That was all that I wanted. I'd made my peace with the end, and I felt very free at that point.

I took out my gun, loaded it up and I stood there and I watched the sunrise.

It's amazing the things you notice when you think that you're just about to die. Standing beside the car I watched long fingers of light creep across the hills as the sun slowly came over the horizon. Shades of pink and orange danced across the clouds and a million tiny rainbows appeared as the sun caught the frost on the leaves and the grass.

I have never seen anything so beautiful in my life. I think for the first time in a long time I was really paying attention.

Any sunrise is a thing of beauty but thinking that this would be my last one made it indescribable.

As it all unfolded, I was paralysed. Everything the sun touched was renewed and revived.

That's when I had my "Oh shit" moment.

I saw hope and how beautiful life could be. It felt like I had been blindfolded and was only just seeing the world for the first time.

There was magic and wonder in the everyday if I could only just see it.

In that moment I realised that I only had one life. I only had one chance to experience everything that life had to offer.

I realised that I didn't have the commitment that I thought that I had. I was chasing oblivion and had made my peace with death. At that moment with that decision resting in my right hand, I realised that for all the shit, all the bad things that amongst all the pain that life could throw at us that there are those indescribable moments of joy.

Watching that sunrise was one of those for me.

I couldn't do it.

It was a moment of clarity. I didn't want to die; I just wanted the pain to end. And deep down I realised that I did have the strength to face it.

That's when I dropped to my knees, and I cried. I sobbed like a child. Deep, hoarse choking sobs like I'd never cried before. I threw my gun away, I couldn't bear to hold onto it. I'd come so close.

It took me a long time before I could stand up again. My body was weak, and I was shaking with my emotions. Relief, grief, hope, sadness, and happiness all at once.

I would love to tell you that this moment magically fixed everything.

It didn't.

It's over 20 years later and I'm still working on my PTSD and night terrors. They'll be with me until the day that I do die. I can't forget what I have seen or what I have experienced.

I'll never forget the betrayal of my mother for leaving me in Bills care after what he had done to her as a child. I can't forget my demons. But I have chosen not to let them stop me from being happy.

After that I went to the station, and I handed in my gun and my resignation.

I chose life.

If those who know me have ever wondered why I am so fixated on sunrises, it's because of this. No matter how dark the night gets, the sun will rise the next day and give us a fresh start.

That's how I have lived my life ever since.

I haven't ever looked back.

CHAPTER 2

It Started With...

"Failure is simply the opportunity to begin again, this time more intelligently."

Henry Ford

HOW DID I GET to that point? How did I let things get so bad?

I was young. I was inexperienced and I never anticipated how badly death and trauma would impact me.

It's taken me years to write this book. Not the actual writing part although that took a while, more the years of introspection and understanding myself well enough to be able to articulate it.

When I look back in time, it was my first encounter with death that later led to the moment when I first realised that I had to quit, to make a change. Unfortunately, at the time I just didn't have the guts to face that truth. I didn't want to be a failure.

I was only a few months out of the Academy when I started working at Smithfield police station. In our first year out, we had to work with Field Training Officers (FTOs) who would act as mentors for us while we did our on-the-job training.

One shift I was rostered to work with Dan. He was a young bloke, only a few years older than me. He was a quiet guy and seemed quite pre-occupied. I didn't mind that, there were some terrible FTOs out there so working with someone who didn't treat you like an idiot was always a plus.

Our shift was going reasonably well until we were given a code one request to head to Trinity Beach. A code one meant lights and sirens and authority to break the traffic laws. It meant get there immediately due to a life-or-death situation.

En route we were given the details. An adult male had been pulled unconscious from the water. No lifeguards were on duty and the ambos were delayed. We were in the area so were only minutes away.

I was driving and this was my first code one. I was young and they'd just given me authority to break every speed and traffic rule to get there. At the Academy they'd put us through driver training and so this was a chance to practice those skills. Wow, it was an adrenaline pumping ride. It's probably the same for every cop, even though code ones mean life and death situations, I never lost the thrill of excitement when I got a code one or two job.

I pulled up near the beach and we raced down to the scene. There was a crowd of people gathered around an adult male lying on his back on the sand. He looked to be in his mid-forties and two locals had started CPR.

We took over the CPR, working in tandem. I did the chest compressions while Dan did the mouth to mouth. This was in the nineties so there were no masks or barriers. Dan didn't hesitate and kept on working on getting breath into old mates lungs.

We kept the CPR going for about five minutes with no change in his status. The ambos arrived and they took over, keeping the resuscitation up while they loaded him into the ambulance.

After they left, I started speaking to the crowd to get some details. One of the guys led me over to a lady sitting nearby. She was distraught. She was in her seventies, Scottish and in Cairns on holiday with her son. They'd left the city centre and were staying for a few days in Trinity Beach to enjoy the sun and the beach.

She told me that her son had some mental health issues. They'd had a bit of an argument while they were on the beach, and he'd become angry and told her that he was going home.

At that point he had walked fully clothed out into the ocean and started swimming, presumably heading for home but in reality, towards Fiji. He wasn't much of a swimmer and so once he'd gotten into deep water, his poor swimming skills plus the weight of his clothes had put him in trouble. Other beachgoers had seen him struggling and sinking and had swum out and pulled him into shore.

He was already unconscious and had swallowed a lot of water.

Dan wasn't anywhere around so I took all her details. I wasn't sure of the protocol as I hadn't dealt with a job like this before. I did the best I could hoping that I hadn't missed anything.

I found Dan at the car and filled him in. He was if anything, more distracted and distant than he had been at the start of the shift but I was engrossed in the new experience so didn't pay much attention. I know that my enthusiasm probably sounds wrong, but I could still count my active duty as a cop in weeks on both hands, so I was completely engaged in the excitement of a real life and death situation. I guess I was also still very optimistic about the outcome and so in the midst of dealing with the situation, reality hadn't quite hit me yet.

Knowing that she'd want to be with her son, we gave the mother a lift to Cairns Base Hospital. The drive took about half an hour and Dan was silent the entire time. I asked her a few questions along the way and tried to keep her calm. It was an awkward drive.

We arrived and took her through to the Accident and Emergency section (A&E) and got her to take a seat in the waiting room while we went and asked for an update.

Unfortunately, we were told that he was pronounced dead on arrival.

That news hit me like a freight train. I rather naively had remained hopeful that our efforts had saved him. It was hard for me to accept that he had died. When the nurse told us this Dan just turned and walked back to the car. He didn't say a word.

That left me with quite a dilemma. I had never delivered a death message and my knees shook with the very thought of delivering that news.

Fortunately, I was saved by the hospital staff. They said that they would tell her and help her with the arrangements.

Oh shit, I was relieved. There was no way that I was emotionally prepared to have that conversation with his mother.

I then went out and found Dan. We got into the car and drove silently back to the station. The only interaction that we had was that along the way Dan asked me to pull over a few times and each time he would open the car door and spit repeatedly. I noticed that his hands were shaking continuously.

When we got back to the station I started to work on the paperwork. Dan went to see the station sergeant and after they spoke for a bit, without a word he grabbed his kit and left.

The station sergeant called me over and told me that Dan was finishing early and that he would supervise my work on the case. The boss gave me details of what I needed to do next and so I started work on my first coronial death file. Cops generally hate them as they're a lot of work. Statements had to be taken from witnesses, the ambos, and the hospital staff. Then there's the autopsy. I'll talk about that process later in this book.

Dan stayed off work for a month or so after that incident and then came back as if nothing had happened. I heard around the station that only a week before the drowning Dan had been transferred back to Smithfield from the remote aboriginal community of Kowanyama. While he had been working there, he'd gotten into a wrestling match with one of the locals who had managed to pull his gun out of its holster. The guy had then held the gun to his head and marched him around town for about three hours until the other cops had calmed him down and negotiated his release.

Poor bastard. Looking back no wonder the drowning shook him.

A few years later, midway through his shift at Smithfield station, Dan walked out into the back carpark and shot himself through the heart with his revolver.

By that time, I was already having trouble sleeping and had developed a few symptoms of stress myself. I'd just come back from three months working in Kowanyama where I'd had my own challenging experiences with the locals. That was when the first thoughts of leaving the job occurred.

Instead, I started looking around at other positions, other departments to work in.

Avoiding the real issues, I buried my head in the sand and tried to find a compromise that I thought would work.

CHAPTER 3

Fear Factor

"Success is not final, failure is not fatal. It is the courage to continue that counts."

Winston Churchill

FEAR COMES IN MANY shapes and forms.
A cornerstone of our training at the academy and the job that
we had signed up for was that we always had to step up. Even
when we were afraid.

On a daily basis we had to step forward. To arrest the suspect.
To stop a brawl. To deliver a death message. We had a job to do,
and we could never afford the luxury of giving in to our own fears
of personal safety. Later on I'll delve deeper into the relationship
between fear and courage.

It's funny but it wasn't the physical danger that I struggled
with. I've been shot at, stabbed (only a little bit), hit by a car

(twice) and punched many times. I'm no brawler, it's just not me but in the thick of those moments I always experienced more of a rush of adrenaline. To this day, over twenty years since I left the job, if someone snatched a bag in front of me the urge to chase them is so ingrained that I act before I think.

Please don't confuse what I've just said with lack of fear. There were many times in my career that I feared for my life and my own physical safety. Times when my legs shook, and my voice quivered. I'm not saying that these things didn't affect me, because they did. I just believe that these were factors that I had been trained to deal with and I had accepted were part of my role. On its own, I don't think that the risks to my personal safety would have pushed me over the edge.

For me, the trigger was all the death and the life-or-death decisions I've ever had to make. All the anxiety and nightmares are from the repeated exposure to fatalities. After a rough period early in the job, one of my old sergeants gave me the advice that everyone has a number, a threshold of how much death each of us could experience before it would overwhelm us. I don't know what my number was, but I knew after I hit it. Oh man I felt it.

Every cop has a different experience. My experience with Dan was the first encounter I'd had with death. From there on, the bodies stacked up until by the time I left the job I'd lost count. I'd speak with other cops who were five years in and only ever been to a couple. While part of it is just the luck of the draw, another part is on me – I never said no to anything.

Throughout this narrative I'll speak about a few individual situations which left their mark on me or taught me more about life and myself, but here I'll talk about what became my greatest trigger.

Throughout my time in the Queensland Police Service, I had worked briefly in other departments, but most of my time was in General Duties. Generals is the aspect of police work that most people encounter. It's the highly reactive patrolling and being tasked with whatever next job came through the radio. You never know what you're going to encounter in Generals, and I loved the diversity and the excitement.

Another area I worked in for a good stint was in the Inquiries section. This was an area of policing where we'd often work on our own and be tasked with following up on various types of inquiries. The ones I came to dread were welfare checks. They generally took the form of, old Mrs Brown hasn't been seen for a few days and there's a bit of a smell around her house, can you stop by and check on her?

The first four years of my service were in the far northern region of Queensland, around Cairns. Cairns has a hot, humid, tropical climate. Things go bad up there very quickly. I can't remember how many welfare checks I did during that period of my work, but it was a lot. Fortunately, most of them were fine.

But the ones who weren't fine were anything but.

When a door knock wouldn't produce an answer, I'd inquire with the neighbours and see if they had any information. Most of the time they were the ones who'd called in the first place.

Sometimes the smell would be bad enough that you could tell from outside the house that there was something bad inside. Other times there'd still be an element of doubt.

Once all other measures had been eliminated, I'd radio in and get approval from the station sergeant to do a house entry. If I was lucky there would be an unlocked door. Most of the time that wasn't the case and I'd find a window to try to climb through.

Frequently these inquiries were for elderly people who lived on their own. But not always, sometimes I'd be checking on the home of a missing person who the family were worried about. Most of these welfare checks I conducted in Cairns seemed to be in older style houses.

I don't know how to describe what it's like to open the door or climb through the window of an old house where inside you expect to find a corpse. For me, this would have my heart hammering in my chest, every nerve fibre ready to leap into action if there was some kind of threat still present. I can't even begin to tell you how glad I am that the series "The Walking Dead" wasn't out at that point, otherwise my imagination would have given me a heart attack in those situations. As it was, I always had a nameless dread of what I'd see or find.

I'm afraid of dead bodies. I've never been comfortable with them. I've seen them in every possible state of trauma, putrefaction and misadventure and I could never overcome my unease around them. I learned to deal with it. I had to because it was my job, but it was a fear that stuck with me.

As I would creep through these strange houses, fumbling to find light switches and not knowing what I was going to find, I would be operating on an insane level of adrenaline.

Sometimes they'd be empty. My god that was always a relief. A couple of times I found dead pets. That was always quite sad.

People can be such dicks, leaving their dog, cat, or bird to die of starvation while they were away on holidays.

But on far too many occasions I'd find the occupant. None of these were good days, but if I was lucky, they were fresh. On the bad days they'd been there for days, decomposing in the heat.

I don't know how to write this without sounding callous about these people. Because I genuinely cared about the fact that these were people like you or I with families, loved ones and people who cared about them. In this instance though, I'm relaying what I was feeling in the role I had to play after their lives were over.

When people had died alone in their beds, I felt some relief for them. I still didn't enjoy my role, but it was comforting to me to believe that someone had simply gone to sleep and not woken up.

Sometimes I'd find them after they'd had a fall. Some of those were so goddam sad. Old people who'd fallen over, broken a limb and not been able to even crawl to get help. A couple of those had days of filth around them which would indicate that they may have waited in pain and fear for hours or days for help to come. Those situations didn't horrify me or give me nightmares they just made me feel so sad. The lost and the lonely souls in our world who die on their own with no-one to turn to.

If you have elderly relatives or neighbours, just keep an eye on them and check in on them regularly. Please.

Quite a few times I'd find obvious suicides. These were often horrible scenes. Overdoses, hangings, a few mutilated through cutting veins etc. and some who'd I'd find in the garage in the car – using a hose to give themselves carbon monoxide poisoning. One of the most inventive, gruesome, and weirdest was the guy who'd used duct tape to position a circular power saw upside down on his work bench with the saw guard taped back, leaving the open spinning blade available for him to lay his neck across. I treated that one as a crime scene and potential murder until after the Criminal Investigation Branch and Scenes of Crimes teams determined that he'd done it on his own. Far out, that did not look like a good way to go.

The deaths which really terrified me were some of the most common. Did you know that heart attacks are often accompanied or perhaps induced by the urge to defecate? It seems to happen regularly in the early hours of the morning when someone will get up to go to the toilet and while emptying their bowels, they'll have a heart attack and pass.

From my perspective, working in Inquiries they were often the hardest to deal with. I would make my way into the house and search room by room, often with that overwhelming stink in my nostrils knowing that there was a corpse slowly decomposing in the hot closed house.

After searching all the other rooms I'd come to the one that I dreaded the most, the smallest room in the house. I would be full of anxiety and hoping like crazy that I wouldn't have to take the next step of finding the body.

You see, I couldn't call in the job as a dead body until I'd both found the body and confirmed that they were in fact deceased. That meant assessing them and making sure that there were no signs of life. More on that in a moment.

In the case of someone who has passed in a toilet, I'd have to approach the toilet door and open it up to check inside. A technical problem for me was that someone passed on the toilet they would often fall forward against the door, making it hard to open and gain entry.

I would find myself turning the handle and pushing my weight against the door only to have something pushing back against me. I'd like you to imagine what it's like to be in a strange house, knowing that what's inside that tiny room was a corpse and often if the smell was anything to go by, that it was in a decomposing state and flyblown. And I couldn't run from this, I had a job to do.

Using all of my strength I would eventually get enough space to get my head into the room. I'd be puffing and panting from the effort, sometimes these people weighed a lot more than I did, but also trying to only breathe through my mouth as the smell was overwhelming. Finally, I'd get a look in there and would often find myself only centimetres away from whoever had passed inside there.

Those moments haunt me. They're some of the faces I see in my dreams.

I really don't mean to disrespect those poor souls. They were people with lives, hopes, and dreams but for me, a young guy in my early twenties alone in their houses, they became my nightmares.

Once I'd found them and confirmed that they were deceased and I can tell you that some of these were very, very dead, then I would get out of the house as quickly as possible and start the process of notifying the family and preparing a report for the coroner.

If I had told anybody who I worked with that I was afraid of dead bodies, I would have been laughed at. There was this image in my mind that I had to live up to, I had to toughen up and be the strong man.

And slowly and inexorably the PTSD took hold of me.

CHAPTER 4

The Moments That Test Us

"Character cannot be developed in ease and quiet. Only through experience of trial and suffering can the soul be strengthened, ambition inspired and success achieved."

Helen Keller

TOWARDS THE END OF my time in the job, as afraid of dead bodies that I'd become, I came to get to know them very well.

Autopsies were a part of the job, particularly working in the Inquiries section as we were responsible for writing all of the non-suspicious coroner files. Every autopsy has to be observed by a police officer as part of the coroners report. I can't recall exactly how many I participated in but it was a lot. In Brisbane the process is very clinical and the cop stands behind a glass screen in the John Tonge medical centre and simply observes the process. Not in Cairns. Up there it was very hands on and a part of our job was to help the medical examiner by weighing various organs for them and help them by bagging the organs and tissue samples as required. Yes, hearts, brains the lot.

In the clinical environment of the hospital mortuary that was quite interesting work, and I learned a great deal about human anatomy during that period of my career. It was sometimes hard going though. Babies, children, waterlogged, decomposed, there were some very hard days in the office spent in that room.

As hard as they were it wasn't that environment that impacted me. It was the in-situ moments that really got to me. Seeing a body on a stainless-steel slab is very clinical and professional. Seeing someone sprawled in their own bodily fluid in their own kitchen or living room is not. It's messy and it's personal.

Exposure to those situations and preparing the medical reports for the coroner helped me to gain a deeper understanding of the causes and process of death. When investigating a sudden death, part of the process is to examine the body for lividity, that purplish bruising which occurs after the heart stops pumping and the blood settles in the lowest parts of the body. Sometimes it can be quite startling and it's easy for a novice to mistake it as a sign of violence.

You also become familiar with the stages of decomposition where the body bloats from the formation of internal gases, often seeing the vascularity standing out in contrast to the whitened skin in the limbs of the victim.

What I'm getting to here is that as experienced as you may get, you can sometimes make mistakes. On one occasion I read too much into some of those signs and made a mistake which almost cost someone their life and at that same time gave me my worst possible nightmare.

A couple of months before the end of my time in the job I was working from Slacks Creek station in the Logan district. I was on a correspondence day in the office when the station sergeant asked me to go do a welfare check on a house only a few blocks from the station. These are supposed to be easy jobs and they hated to waste an operational crew on them, so it made sense to send me.

Well, to everyone but me.

By that stage I was only a month or two away from the end of my time in the job. Of course, nobody at work knew what I was going through, but the PTSD had me firmly in its grip.

A solo welfare check at this point was one of my worst possible nightmares.

The house was only a couple of blocks away, so I walked over there rather than taking one of the cars. When I arrived one of the neighbours was there to meet me in the driveway. He seemed like a nice old bloke. He said that the elderly lady who lived there hadn't been seen for a few days and that was unusual for her. He knew her quite well and she hadn't spoken about going away, and her cat had been coming to his house for food.

I had a look around the house and the front door was unlocked. I radioed the station and got approval to enter.

Inside the house was dim and cool (thank God it wasn't the usual body bakery temperature). I went through the front lounge room and the bedroom and fortunately I couldn't smell anything, that was promising.

My heart was racing, and the adrenaline was coursing through my body. One of the joys of PTSD is that a triggering situation will cause that surge and I was in full fight or flight mode.

Going off topic here but every time a cop shoots someone in the course of their duty there is endless debate afterwards over the use of lethal force. Although I had years of experience at that point in my career, me walking around in that state of hyper-vigilance with a loaded gun on my hip was an accident waiting to happen. I'm just so very lucky that during that period of my life I didn't make particular mistake. Whenever I see a police shooting hit the news I can't help wondering about what that cop was experiencing at that moment in their life.

Back to my story. Finally, I made it through to the kitchen and as I entered, I saw a pair of legs lying next to the dining room table. As I came into the room, I could see that it was an elderly lady who looked like she was in the early stage's postmortem. She was a large woman, and I could see that her dress was up, and she had very evidently fouled herself. Her legs were white with heavy vascularity, and I could see what looked like lividity on both. It was a sad scene but in my heightened state of anxiety it was quite a relief to find that it wasn't particularly traumatic.

I stepped back into the kitchen and radioed into the station to start organising the next steps in having the body removed.

Then I too shit myself. She rolled over.

I can't even begin to describe how this was my worst nightmare. A corpse moving in front of me. FUCK! Every fibre of my being told me to run. It was all I could do to stop myself from drawing my gun. Like I said above, I was on a hair trigger.

I realised then that I hadn't checked for signs of life. She wasn't dead!

I raced to the body and checked her pulse. It was very faint, but it was there, and her respiration was shallow, but she was breathing. I jumped back on the radio and called for an ambulance asap. I rolled her into the recovery position, placed a pillow under her head and started talking to her. She remained unconscious until the ambos got there and they prepped her and took her off to the hospital.

She lived. That story ended well but … I blamed myself for the near miss.

One of the most important parts of our job was to step forward even when you're afraid. I should have checked her body for signs of life. I hadn't because I was afraid and as a result, I made a bad decision.

I never told anyone about that mistake. I was too afraid to admit my weakness. Time and age has me realising that not admitting that my fear was impacting my work was far worse than the actual fear itself. Mistakes like that can cost lives.

Too afraid to speak up, I continued on but tortured myself with guilt. I felt guilty for the fear itself and for what that fear was doing to my work.

CHAPTER 5

One Bad Decision Can Cost You Everything

"It's okay to make mistakes sometimes. Everyone does – even grown-ups! That's how we learn."

Todd Parr

A FTER THAT INCIDENT I felt like I needed to get away from the reactive work for a while and so I asked the boss if I could work in the Inquiries section for a bit. Yes, there was the risk of having to go to sudden deaths, but that was lower risk than the wild ride of Generals where you never knew what you'd be dealing with on a daily basis. I needed a break and some sort of routine.

A lot of the Inquiries work at Slacks Creek station was following up on Warrants of Commitment. The system has changed since but at the time if you failed to pay a fine on time then the state would issue a (WOC) Warrant of Commitment for the police to enforce. Put simply a WOC gave us the power to demand either the money or the body, which was our term for if you didn't have the money to pay the fine when we knocked on your door or pulled you over, we would simply arrest you under the WOC. From there we would take you to the watchhouse where you would serve one day in custody for every thirty dollars that you owed.

They were straightforward, most were small fines from unpaid speeding tickets or similar. The average punter would produce the cash quickly once they realised that we'd be taking them back to the watchhouse.

We had hundreds of WOCs in our area and so one of the easiest tasks in Inquiries was to simply grab a stack of them in a certain area and just go visit the houses. I started doing just that. Remember, this was pre-internet, so I'd check our internal database for the latest driver's license address and then the phone book for address details. Once I had a pile to work from, I'd head out and knock on a few doors.

Don't get me wrong, sometimes they'd get pretty confrontational but that wasn't a part of the job I had any issues with. I steadily worked my way through my list until I came to one that caught my eye.

Let's call her Beth. Beth had an outstanding WOC for five thousand dollars. She'd been to court over a string of offences and had narrowly avoided jail time but received that hefty fine. Of course, she hadn't paid a cent towards it and all my searches showed that she lived near our station.

While we would refer to executing WOCs as going for "the money or the body" we weren't draconian about it. If someone had a substantial fine, we'd often use the threat of arrest and time inside to get them onto a payment plan. Really, we tended to view this work as administrative rather than punitive.

I drove to Beths house with the intention of getting her to make a first instalment and then start chipping away at the fine.

The house she was living in was uninspiring about her financial condition. There was a lot of rubbish in her overgrown front yard. From the state of the place I would imagine that her landlord would have been close to making a decision about keeping her on as a tenant. The place was a mess.

I knocked on the door and a woman in her mid-forties answered, she fit the profile. I told her my name and asked if she was indeed Beth. "Yeah, what's it to you?"

"Well Beth, if you recall from your time in court, a fine was issued to you and unfortunately you haven't honoured that commitment. Consequently, a warrant has been issued which commands me to demand some payment towards that fine or alternatively to arrest you."

"I'm not paying a fucking cent. You dogs can get fucked."

Sigh....

"Beth, I'm not asking you to pay the full amount but now that I'm here we're faced with two alternatives. Either you make arrangements to make some payment towards this commitment or I have to arrest you. If we do that then you'll be taken to the watchhouse at Beenleigh, where you'll be held in custody either until you've served your term of one hundred and sixty-seven days or someone comes in to pay whatever amount is outstanding at that point at a rate of thirty dollars a day. What's it going to be?"

She held up her hands. "Then go on and arrest me you cunt. Take a woman out of her home you fucking dog."

"Are you sure that's the way you want this to go Beth?"

"Go on, stop fucking around you dog. Either fucking hand-cuff me now or fuck off out of my house."

"Okay then Beth. You're under arrest. Grab your keys and lock the house up as I'll now be taking you to the watchhouse at Beenleigh."

That set her off. There was a lot more of the same language and abuse. I held my tongue and just kept my cool. At this point she was just venting; it was common in those circumstances, and I didn't see her as a threat. It wasn't how I'd anticipated this encounter going but I wasn't overly concerned.

"Well, you dog cunt, I've got my fucking period. Are you going to let me get my tampons and take a piss first before you lock me up?"

Okay, so that obviously posed a bit of a problem. Once I'd uttered those words "you're under arrest" I should have called for back-up and asked for a female officer to come to the location.

Why didn't I?

I don't really know. I think at that stage I knew that I wasn't coping, and I was desperate to not let anyone know that. I've spent many years reflecting on that decision, and I really think that I was overcompensating to prove that I was fine, I'd got this under control.

I know that in the past I never would have made that mistake. I would have called for help.

Instead, I told her that she could use the toilet with the door closed and I would stand outside.

There are reasons why we search prisoners before we take them into custody and there are reasons why we then keep them under observation. I was about to learn that lesson the hard way.

She went to the toilet. Sorted herself out and then came out. I told her that if she came quietly, I wouldn't need to handcuff her, and she just shrugged and walked with me to the police car.

I sat her in the back seat behind the plexiglass barrier and then I started driving to the Beenleigh watchhouse. I radioed in my location and that I was returning with one female in custody. Out of habit I kept an eye on her in the rear vision mirror. Along the way she put her head down and I figured that this was because she was resigned to her fate.

We arrived at the watchhouse, and I pulled up at the roller door. I hit the intercom, and they opened the roller door and I drove in.

Inside, one of the watchhouse staff was there to meet me and I jumped out to get her out of the car. As soon as I saw her I could tell something was wrong. Her head was lolling to the side and froth from her mouth had spilled down her dress. I grabbed her and started shaking her, but she was unresponsive.

"Fuck, she's taken something." I patted her pockets and found an empty pill bottle. No label.

George, the watchhouse Sergeant said "Mate, get her to the hospital. We can't take her like that." Tell me something I don't know.

I jumped back in the car and gunned it out the driveway. I radioed in and asked for the duty Sergeant. I quickly told him what had happened and asked for a code to get to Logan Hospital. A code was authorisation to suspend speed limits and road rules. Code three was proceed normally, code two was lights and sirens – you can exceed the speed limit and run red lights but proceed with caution and finally code one was, someone's going to die if you don't get there in time, do whatever you have to do.

He gave me a code one.

As soon as I'd backed out of the watchhouse I flicked on my lights and sirens and raced out of Beenleigh. Once I hit the M1 Highway I accelerated averaging about one hundred and fifty even after I took the Loganholme turnoff onto the Logan Motorway. The whole time I was yelling at her, "Don't you fucking die on me Beth, come on you bitch, don't fucking die."

The total drive took me about fifteen minutes. It felt like eternity before I pulled up on the ramp outside Accident and Emergency.

I was just about to get out of the car when I was jerked forward with a violent crash. I turned around and an ambulance had reversed into me.

FUCK!

I jumped out of the car and ran to the ambos. They started to talk but I stalled them and said, "Don't worry about the cars, I've got a woman who's overdosed in the back, I need to get her in there asap."

They both jumped into action, and we grabbed Beth and got her onto a trolley. The nurses started doing their thing and I stepped back to give them room. I gave them all her details and the background on the situation. They took her straight in and the last I saw of her they were starting to intubate her.

I spoke with the ambos and took all their details and then I made the dreaded call. Back to the station. I'd had what was known as a "departmental", that's when you manage to crash a cop car. With any departmental the duty Sergeant had to visit the scene and of course there was lots of paperwork.

I'll pause for a moment here to say that my stress and anxiety was through the roof. My heart was hammering in my chest, and I felt like I couldn't breathe. It was about an hour later when the duty Sergeant rocked up. The damage to both the police car and the ambulance wasn't too bad but it still required a report and he had to interview me. We went through it all and he wasn't overly worried about the Departmental. The ambos had both admitted that my car was stationary when they had reversed into it.

Then sarge turned his attention to Beth.

"Mate, you've got yourself a problem here. Do you reckon she's going to make it?"

I'd spoken with the doctor in the long wait for the sarge to arrive. He'd said it was fifty-fifty, he wasn't very confident. They'd pumped her stomach, but it just depended on how much had gotten into her system. We were still trying to work out exactly what she'd taken.

I said, "I don't know, the doc said it could go either way."

"You know that if she dies, it's a death in custody."

Yep, I knew that all too well. I'd been involved in a couple of other deaths in custody while I worked in the watchhouse, they were literally one of our worst nightmares.

You see, once you've taken someone into your custody, you have a duty of care. If you're found to have breached your duty of care, in addition to whatever internal discipline you may face you are open to criminal prosecution for manslaughter. I've had mates go through this. The process takes years and can be devastating, both personally and professionally. You never realise when you sign up for this job that a bad day at work could have you in jail for the rest of your adult life.

I had breached my duty of care. I should have called for a female officer and searched her before she went to the toilet. If she died, not only would I have to live with that memory, but there was also a very real chance that I would be charged with manslaughter, stood down from work and have to endure the years of due process before a trial in court. And then if the verdict was bad…

Every scenario was running through my head. I could barely breathe.

After a few hours of no improvement on her condition my shift was coming to an end. I drove back to the station and finished up my paperwork for the night.

In the months leading up to this event I'd separated from Sandra, who later became my wife. I never really opened up to her about what I was going through and while I kept a mask on my stress, every little thing had escalated into an argument, and I had become cold and distant. I had moved out and we were separated.

I had moved in with a friend, Sharon and was staying in her spare room.

When I got home, Sharon was out for the night and so I was alone with my thoughts. I sat in the lounge room with a bottle of wine and slowly drank and cried. Every hour I called the hospital for an update on Beth. No improvement.

I can't describe the agony of that night. Every thought crossed my mind including suicide. I was so alone and so lost. I would not wish a night like that on anybody. Eventually about four am I passed out on the couch.

I woke up about six thirty, confused and hoping that it had just been a nightmare. It didn't take me long to remember that it was anything but.

My first call was to the hospital. Beth had stabilised. She had returned to consciousness.

She was alive.

There was such a surge of emotion. Relief was mixed with tormented guilt. I had fucked up and fucked up bad.

I will always have to live with the fact that although she made many wrong decisions, I could have been responsible for Beth's death. Adding this next layer of guilt onto my existing anxiety started to tear me apart. I couldn't stop thinking about my mistakes but I felt like I had to push through and stay strong.

CHAPTER 6

The Final Straw

"Resilience is very different than being numb. Resilience means you experience, you feel, you fail, you hurt. You fall. But, you keep going."

Yasmin Mogahed

THE FINAL STRAW FOR me occurred only weeks after this. What happened here wasn't my fault, I couldn't have done anything differently, but I would see his face in my dreams for years afterwards.

I had returned to working back in Generals and had just started working night shifts. Ten pm to six ams. One night Sergeant Tracey and I started work at ten pm (or actually at nine fifty – Tracey was old school which meant that if you started on time, you were late!) We were given our first job before we even left the station.

A thirty-year old male had committed suicide by hanging himself in his unit. A friend had just found him. When we arrived, the scene was pretty standard. It turned out that this guy had cancer and had decided to beat the tumour to it. It was sad but it was a very routine job for both of us, so as callous as it may sound, neither of us were unduly affected by it. Well maybe we were but were just desensitised by then. We called for the morticians and went about getting his details and finding information about his next of kin so that we could notify them.

We were finishing up at the scene when we received a call on the radio to go code one to a motor vehicle incident. You'll recall that code one was the most urgent of codes, it meant get there by any means, someone's dying.

We raced to the scene. In transit, we were given more details. A car had run a red light and been hit by another car. The car had rolled and there were multiple fatalities with an entrapment. The ambos and firies were tied up at other incidents so we would be on our own until they could get units free.

When we arrived, the scene was a mess. A heavily damaged car was upright on one side of the intersection. The damage to its sides and roof indicated that it had rolled. Another car was off to the side, front end damaged but didn't seem to be in bad shape.

We later pieced together the story from the driver of the other car and the tyre tracks. That confirmed that the car that ended up rolling had run the red light and the other guy had t-boned it, causing it to roll a few times and end up where we found it. The driver of the other car was shaken but ok. When we arrived, he was helping another guy with the entrapment.

The scene was a complete mess. There was a sad lesson here about seatbelts.

The first of the passengers had been thrown from the vehicle, hit the road and somehow had lost the back part of his skull, he was very evidently already dead. The second passenger had also been thrown clear, but he had hit the metal guardrail at significant speed and the impact had impaled him into the guardrail through his left shoulder, smashing through his torso and effectively tearing him apart to the groin. He was still in-situ when we arrived and again, very obviously dead.

The driver had obviously been the only one of the three with his seat belt on. He was still in his seat, but the front of the car was crushed, and his legs were trapped. He was very conscious and screaming for help. The driver of the other car and another bloke were trying to free him from the wreckage.

Flames were also coming out from under the bonnet of the car. Tracey got our small fire extinguisher out and worked on the fire while I joined the two blokes who were trying to free the driver. The driver's side door was wrecked and wouldn't open but the main issue was that the front of the car had crumpled. He was pinned in place by the steering wheel and underside of the dashboard. He said that his legs hurt but he didn't think they were broken. He seemed to be in good shape.

We were working frantically. The bonnet of the car was wrecked and wouldn't open which meant that Tracey couldn't put the fire out. She could attack whatever flames came out from the gaps, but the fire kept going.

I've spoken before about my mental and physiological reactions to things. This wasn't a triggering moment. I was working flat out to solve the problem and I didn't have any time to panic. My head was clear, we just needed to find a way to get this boy out of the car.

Time was against us though. That fire would not go out. Tracey had tried her best and the fire extinguisher was out. She'd called again for the firies and they were still ten minutes away.

When flames started to come out of the dashboard of the car the other guys backed away. I was using all of my strength to try to force the door open with a tyre iron, hoping that with the door open we could slide him sideways and out. I kept talking to him trying to reassure him and he was crying and grabbing hold of my arms.

He was seventeen years old.

The flames were in the car, there was petrol all over the road.

He kept screaming and begging for my help. The fire got hotter and more intense.

It was only when his clothes caught fire that Tracey pulled me away from him.

I couldn't turn away and I just kept yelling "I'm sorry, I'm sorry," to him as the tears ran down my face.

I watched him burn to death.

I can never forget his face as he screamed for help. I've had people die in front of me before, bleeding out from car accidents, slit wrists and drownings but this was the worst that I've ever seen.

Eventually the firies arrived and they put the flames out. By that stage the boy was dead and he was just a charred corpse.

They ironically used the "jaws of life" to free his body for the undertaker.

We collected IDs from the other two victims to start the long process of working through this accident.

With any sudden death we had to meet the undertakers at the medical facility, in this case the John Tonge centre and check the bodies in, take their photographs and then notify the next of kin. We'd completely forgotten the earlier suicide so by this time when we go there, we had to go through the process with all four bodies.

One of our required tasks was to take a polaroid photo of the deceased for identification purposes. For one of these boys that wasn't going to work. Suicides by shotgun to the head, fires and decomposition, especially in water made it very hard to identify the bodies. You see, the easiest method for identifying a body is to have a relative look at either a photo or the body itself and positively identify who they are.

So then started a long morning of death messages. Waking up families and telling them that someone they loved had passed.

We did the suicide first. His next of kin was his sister and she took it pretty stoically. Apparently, he'd told his family that he wasn't going to let the cancer take him.

Then the first of the young boys. This guy was the guy who'd lost the back of his skull. He was seventeen years old. Around four thirty in the morning we woke his dad up to tell him the news. There's never an easy way to tell a parent that they've just lost a child, and this went as expected. Once he had passed the initial shock, denial then an immediate outburst of grief followed.

We had to ask him about who his son had been out with. He gave us the name of one of the other boys, the sixteen year old passenger. We organised for his sister to come over and stay with him as we didn't want to leave him alone with his grief.

We arrived at the second boys house at about six am. On this occasion we spoke with both his mother and father. We asked for a photo of him to confirm before we broke the news and as always, I hated seeing the agony in their faces as they desperately hoped that we were wrong or had a different boy. The moment they realised that it was indeed their son, when their hearts broke, and their lives changed direction forever.

I can't describe what this is like. It's fucking horrible.

Finally, we went to the last house. The car was registered to a man in his forties, who we believed was the boy's father. It was about seven am when we arrived, and he was beside himself. His son had borrowed his car the night before and he had no idea who he was out with. He didn't really know any of his sons friends and so he had been ringing around desperately trying to find where his son was.

It was again, as expected. Absolutely heart-breaking.

This was harder again. Each of the other two families had wanted to go to the morgue to see their children and we had given them details of how to arrange this. This father wanted to do the same thing. How do you tell a father that you watched his only son die in fire and agony? That his body is unrecognisable and that to see him would haunt him forever.

Tracey and I were exhausted. When we got back to the station, we sat in the meal room and didn't speak for a long time.

Tracey was a thirty plus year veteran, heading towards retirement. I noticed that her hands were shaking continuously.

Then we packed up our stuff and we went home.

Rationally, I know that I couldn't have done anything more to try to save him. That didn't stop me from dwelling on it. I'd made so many mistakes recently that my confidence in myself was shot. I was so full of self-doubt that I started to obsess that it was my fault.

That somehow, I could have done better, I could have changed the outcome.

I couldn't stop seeing his face.

If I tried to sleep, I'd see his face. Already suffering from chronic lack of sleep I started spiralling. I was living in a fog of sleep deprivation and self-loathing. I couldn't bear to look in a mirror because I expected to see his face looking back at me. It was a horrible enough experience to go through but when you start blaming yourself for it as well, it took me to the edge.

Have you ever been pulled over by a cop and had them lose their shit at you? The angry cop who seems to take your traffic law infringement personally? If it ever happens to you consider this…

Around a week after that incident I was working with another young cop and our patrol took us through that intersection. It would have been impossible for me not to flinch as we got close, the memory was so raw. As we approached the intersection the lights turned red and the car in front of us took the chance and ran through the red light. Right in front of our police car!

I saw red. I flicked on the lights and sirens and raced after them. They pulled over quickly and so I jerked our car to a stop behind them and immediately strode up to the drivers side window.

I have no recollection of what I said to them. I raged and I yelled at them. My heart was pounding in my chest and I'm sure that I was spitting at them in the heat of my anger. I just remember the faces of the male driver and his female passenger as they recoiled in shock and probably fear.

Lance, my partner grabbed me by the arm and pulled me away. I can't remember what he said to me but I think he was asking if I'd gone mad, that we'd get a complaint against us. I was his Field Training Officer, he had about three months service at that stage.

I told him to write them a ticket and I went and sat back in the drivers seat, shaking and trying to hold back my tears. I refused to let myself cry.

A couple of days after that I took that drive out to Stanthorpe.

CHAPTER 7

Finding Resilience

"Do not judge me by my success, judge me by how many times I fell down and got back up again."

Nelson Mandela

THAT DEAR READER, IS the story of how I reached that tipping point. Part two of this book will talk about what happened after then and will focus on change. For now I'd like to discuss the concept of resilience and what I learned after looking back at my journey to the edge. I've titled this chapter Finding Resilience. I believe that we all have it in us, we simply need to find where it lies.

For me it was when I hit the edge. I was ready to tap out but at the last moment realised that I wasn't quite ready to give it all up. What did I learn from that?

For a start, I've had to change how I view myself and the world. I've learned to be realistic about who I am and most importantly to know who I am not. The word authenticity means so much in that context. It's about knowing who we are and accepting our own strengths and weaknesses. For me it was accepting that I'm not a cop, not as I was then anyway.

Knowing myself has made me happy.

It's over twenty years since that morning in Stanthorpe. I've seen a couple of thousand sunrises since then. I've built a career that I'm proud of, I have a wife and a family who I love and I'm lucky enough now to work in a field that I love, doing work which I'm passionate about.

I've had so many amazing days. I've travelled, I've loved, and I've laughed.

I've had shit days as well. Days when I've lost and days when I have cried.

But funnily enough, after hitting rock bottom I somehow now appreciate the shit days as well. Because no matter how bad they are, there's always something for me to learn or some good amongst them.

So here's what I've learned from hitting rock bottom.

On Failure

Previously I wrote that I had tried to live my life by a code. I've seen it in gyms, as an inspirational poster, in many different forms. In order to succeed we're told that "Failure is not an option."

I was wrong. Don't believe that.

Failure can be ok. We can bounce back and learn when we fail. While writing this book I spoke with a close friend about what she would change if she could go back in time and talk to her younger self during the hard times. She said nothing. She said they were shit times and they sucked, but that to be the person she is today she had to experience them. When she said that, I realised that she was right. I hate that I experienced what I have, but it has made me who I am today.

However, in the future I will strive harder to be myself and not who I think others want me to be. I have learned to accept failure and to move on. It has been such an important lesson.

The Role of Hope in Resilience

The first thing I learned about building my own resilience is about endurance. We're more capable than we think we are.

In the 1950's, Curt Richter was a professor at John Hopkins University. He had a hypothesis about hope and endurance. In a series of cruel experiments he put rats in buckets to see how long they would swim before they drowned. In some cases it was only minutes. He then repeated the experiment with similar rats and waited for the moment when he could see that they were giving up, then he rescued them and let them recover. When he then put those rats back into the water they would keep swimming for days before they gave up.

I hate the cruelty of that experiment but the lesson is something I believe applies to us all.

I think that we all have tremendous endurance, we just don't realise it until we are down in the mud getting tested. In order to keep going, we have to have a belief, a hope, that it will somehow get better. Or, for me it is curiosity.

After hitting my lowest point and then coming back from it, I realise that you never know what's around the corner. Leading up to that moment I felt like it was completely hopeless, that I was out of options. It turns out that it wasn't hopeless and that I did have options. I just couldn't see that at the time.

So, whenever I am feeling that a moment is hopeless I lean into the curiosity. What is around the corner?

If I give up, I'll never know.

I run a lot now. When I am feeling low on energy, like I just can't run any further, then I take a different route. I do this to let the curiosity take over. To find out what's around that next bend or over that next hill. When I do that I find that I can find the energy to keep on going.

I never focus on the finish line. That goal is too distant, too far away. Instead I concentrate on the next corner, the next hill, the next tree. I run to it and then I feel great that I made it, so I then look for the next goal.

I feel that life is like that, especially when it gets tough. We can set the big goals, but then when we're in the mud, feeling low, we can shift our focus to just taking that next step. Put all of our energy and attention into getting to that next milestone even if it's only centimetres away. Then find the next one. Repeat and repeat again and step by step we get to the finish line.

That's what I have learned about my own endurance. I have it, I just can't let the bigger picture overwhelm me and so I focus on the smaller goals to get there.

Find something to hope for.

Warning Signs

When I reflect back to the years and months leading up to Stanthorpe I realise that there were plenty of warning signs that I either missed or ignored. The signs that told me that I wasn't coping.

I was young and not that self-aware. I think that until we've faced these types of crises that we won't realise our own warning signs.

Since Stanthorpe I've seen those warning signs appear plenty of times. Fortunately I've learned to recognise them. For me they can be:

- Sleeplessness
- Irritability
- Inability to concentrate
- Desire to hibernate or retreat from social activity
- Sense of being overwhelmed

The thing is, unless we're born ultra wealthy, most of us must live and work in the real world. Work, life and relationships can be stressful. Since leaving the police service I've worked hard in my career and sometimes under very stressful conditions.

When I notice my warning signs, I take additional steps to care for myself. I've learned to lean on my wife, my friends and the people who I trust to support me. I've learned to take the time out to do the things which help me to regain my energy and get myself back on track.

Self Care

From the above I have learned to care for myself. To love myself and to make my well-being a priority.

I read something once and I haven't been able to find and credit the original source, but it rang so true for me:

> *"Most of the time we feel burnt out and tired not because we've done too much, but because we've done too little of what makes us come alive."*

I do something for myself every morning. Whether that's a walk, a run, the gym or yoga. I make time every day to do something with my physical body while I let my mind wander and prepare for the day ahead. I've found that this helps me by giving me a sense of achievement each morning, "Hooray! I did something to maintain my body!" but also it gives me time to get my thoughts in order and ready for a day of work so that when I start work I've almost already pre-written emails in my head or mentally prepared scripts for the hard conversations.

Our bodies and minds are like cars, if we don't service them regularly then we can't be surprised if they break down on us, right?

My Mantra

Since that time I now wrap all of the above up into my mantra. In any endeavour I undertake, I repeat to myself four words. I use them in my work, in my fitness and everything else I strive for. In fact, I repeated them daily to myself while writing this book.

Insistence, persistence, resistance and consistence.

Insistence: Insist on making what's important to you a priority. Don't let it get pushed to the side. If you want to improve your fitness, insist on that being a priority. If you need to take time out, learn to say no to others and take the time that you need to recharge. Insist on making yourself a priority.

Persistence: Work hard towards your goals. You will get tired; you will fall. Keep on getting up, keep on trying. If it's worth achieving, then it will take hard work and that takes persistence. Keep trying. But, remember the next word, resistance.

Resistance: Amongst it all resist the temptation of pride. Know your limits and know when to walk away. Resist the urge to fill a bottomless hole. Failure is ok if you've tried your best. I know that this sounds counter to persistence but it's not. You will know in yourself when you have to accept failure. Be honest with yourself.

Consistence: Be consistent in your efforts. Set aside time each day, each week to work on whatever is important to you. Don't procrastinate or put it off. If you put in the work, then inch by inch you will get there. One day at the gym will not change your body. One year of three hundred and sixty-five days in the gym will totally change you. Be consistent in keeping your goals and your well-being a priority. Get back up when you fall.

These four words summarise what I have learned about my resilience.

Resilience is learning how to cope when life challenges you. To me, that means when the struggle gets hard, that you should double down and focus on keeping yourself well. Being insistent on caring for yourself and what you need.

I'm not equating self-care with selfishness. The two are not the same. The best analogy I can give is the airline metaphor. When those oxygen masks drop, fit your own first and make sure that you're okay. Not through selfishness, but because once you're okay, then you can then help others.

Since my lowest moment I have focused on getting myself right. On self-care and understanding what I need to do to not just survive, but to thrive. Caring for myself, trying hard and knowing how to accept failure.

Most of all I have focused on allowing myself to be me, not any other person's perception of me.

I hope that these words come to mean something for you.

PART 2

Owning Change

Part of my journey has always been about
absorbing and integrating the things that other
have taught me that make me more.
Another part has been throwing off the things
that others have taught to me which made me
less.
The hardest part was learning to tell
the difference between the two.

CHAPTER 8

What Happened Next?

"It's not the strongest of a species that survive, nor the most intelligent, but the ones most resilient and responsive to change."

Charles Darwin

I READ SOMETHING ONCE WHICH really resonated for me about that time. I've never been able to track down the source, but to paraphrase it, "I realised then that I didn't want to die, I just wanted the life I was living then to end."

Rather than kill myself, I had to change. First, I had to exit from the Queensland Police Service. I wouldn't wish that process on anyone.

I want to discuss that process in this context because there was a part of the process that forced me to change. In order to complete my exit, I had to open up and to speak about my trauma. That scared the hell out of me. I didn't want anyone to know my shame.

Simply quitting would have been the easiest pathway. But I was wrecked. I knew that it was going to take me time to find another job, another career. With a mortgage and a car loan I would have survived about three weeks if I just quit. Foolishly thinking that it would help me to get help and support, I reached out to the Police Union and told them of what was happening for me. That triggered a process for a "medical retirement."

I knew and I guess you can tell from above that I was done. But in order to be able to give myself some time and resources to get back on my feet they had to actually diagnose me with a medical condition and the onus was on me to prove that I wasn't capable of continuing to work in the QPS.

Spoiler alert, I've previously spoken about having PTSD, so you know what the diagnosis was. It was also about proving that that was enough to prevent me from being able to return to work. So that meant first having a few sessions with our human services officer who was an inhouse psychologist. That meant opening up about what I had been through and making myself vulnerable.

There were no secrets about what was going on. There should have been, it should have remained confidential, however within forty-eight hours, I'm sure that everyone in the station knew what was going on. The stigma from that is enormous. That prospect also scared the hell out of me. I knew that it was coming but I was still hurt and disappointed by how quickly I was on the outer.

In the wild, herds of animals will often distance themselves from the lame or the weak, turning their backs on them and forcing them out on their own. It's a survival instinct, where they know that the predators will take the sacrifice and leave the rest of the herd alone.

The QPS was no different.

There were a couple of beautiful souls who quietly reached out to me at the time to see how I was going. Sergeant Tracey was one of them, she was tough as nails but with a big heart. In the many years since, other cops have since fallen from the same or similar reasons and often they will reach out to me. I'm always there for them. My door is always open.

So… the process started, and it was off to see the HSO.

This was the first time in my service that I engaged in any form of counselling other than getting drunk together after a shift.

I can't remember her name. She was a really gentle person and she was pretty empathetic. Really, her job was to see if they could patch me up, give me some light duties for a while and then get me back on the road. I don't know if it's wrong for me to say it, but I knew that wasn't an option, it simply wasn't going to work. I was too damaged by that stage. Counselling and medication may have helped me to cope better but I knew in myself that if I stayed the job would have killed me, or I would have killed me.

But they have to try.

I knew that I had to speak up and I was determined to just give the clinical details. Just enough for her to see that I had been through some rough stuff but not enough for me to open up and spill out my feelings. I wasn't ready for that change. I had spent so long pushing everyone away that I was terrified of making myself vulnerable.

She'd been given my file and started the conversation with some pleasantries. She did a pretty good job of making me feel comfortable, but I was on edge, and it didn't help that underneath it all I felt that we were operating at cross purposes.

The conversation went south when she said "I understand that you've recently had a pretty traumatic experience at work. Perhaps we could start by talking about that."

I snorted a bit at that and said "I'm sorry, but you'll have to narrow it down. Which one are you talking about?"

She looked at the file and she said "I've only got one incident noted here, the recent passing of a teenage boy. How do you feel about that?"

I said "I'm confused, but if it's the job I'm thinking about there were three teenagers killed. Is that the one you're talking about?"

She was definitely feeling a bit out of her depth at that point because she started flicking through pages of the file and then said "I don't see mention of any others, I'm talking about the suicide of a teenage boy about two weeks ago."

It took a moment before it clicked. In between Beth and the car fire, I'd been to the suicide of a fourteen year old aboriginal boy in Woodridge. His family had found him hanging from a tree in the back yard. It was a sad job, very emotional with the family all around while we had to cut him down, but I'd experienced so much that this had been forgotten about within a few days.

That sounds fucking terrible, doesn't it? How do you become so desensitised that the suicide of a teenager doesn't move your trauma dial?

It's relative is all that I can say. I can look at it objectively as a horrific, emotive event in your workday but for me, by that point I had seen so much worse so often that it didn't even register.

I get sad thinking about that now. I'll venture off topic for a moment.

Recently I caught up with an ex Scenes-of-Crime Investigator. The SOC guys were the people who turn up and take photos, do fingerprints and all that sort of stuff. On a lot of cop shows they'll call them forensic officers.

He and I shared some stories and had been in some of the same places with similar experiences. Both of us had worked Inquiries up north, so we got talking about how most people wouldn't believe that in the nineties the observing cop would have to get hands on in post-mortems. Talking with him I remembered how desensitised we'd become. Times when lunch breaks were short so I would scoot from an autopsy with bags of tissue samples and organs in my car to transport to the pathologists but have to stop by the KFC drive thru along the way to get lunch.

It seems surreal to me now. And it seems wrong. But that was just how it was for us.

Anyway, I digress. In response to her question about the incident I burst out laughing "You're kidding me right, that's what they think tipped me over the edge?"

She leaned into it "Wouldn't you say that the suicide of a teenager is pretty traumatic?"

I tried to explain to her. "Yes, any suicide is tragic. But, with no disrespect to the dead that one was pretty straightforward. Very sad, but we didn't even have to deliver a death message to the family as they were the ones who found him. From my perspective, it wasn't traumatic other than by the cumulative effect of yet another dead body at work for me."

I don't know how she took that one, but she paused a bit.

"There's obviously a bit to discuss here, you thought I was referring to the death of three teenagers, can you tell me about that?"

Yes. I had a lot to say about that.

I told her about the burning car.

She sat and listened, taking a few notes as I spoke. I told the whole story, very clinically, and left nothing out.

She started to ask questions about it and was really focusing upon it. My frustration started to build. At that point I only had a very loose grip on my anger, it was always simmering.

"Look, you're focusing on that incident. It was fucking terrible. But the worst of it is that was just the latest in a string of shitstorms that I've been to. I've got years' worth of this shit in my head and never once have I spoken to a shrink or a counsellor. It's never been offered to me and then I'm finally sent here to talk to you, and they think it's because some stupid kid necked himself."

Then I unloaded. I listed incident after incident that I'd been to, where I'd never been debriefed, never offered counselling, never found a way to try to deal with the horror, fear and sadness I'd encountered.

What about Kate? What about Anna? What about Mark? What about me?

Sadness always came with the anger. I would lash out and then I would get sad. As I spoke and the words poured out of me, my eyes filled with tears, and I cried. There was so much in my head. I've told you above of the events that happened at the end of my service but there was so much more along the way. I'd gone into this session with a resolve to be clinical but in that moment, I opened up and let it out.

Even now, when I sit back and contemplate my time in the job, I can barely believe the things that I saw and how I had managed to cope with them.

How I felt when Dan shot himself.

Sitting by the side of the road cradling a middle-aged bloke who had been disembowelled in a traffic accident. Holding on to him and telling him it would be alright while he tried to pick the gravel off his intestines while he tried to pull them back into his gut. Praying for the ambos to get there in time. Hurt, angry, frustrated and confused when they didn't and feeling so fucking helpless as he passed away in my arms. Going home to my poor fiancé at the time and then getting irrationally angry when she pointed out that I had a bit of body tissue on my stained shirt, so me ripping my shirt off and burning it in the back yard.

Walking along train tracks with a bag and gloves and picking up the pieces of the two teenagers who had lain down across the train lines. Their young bodies torn apart and strewn over one hundred metres of train tracks while the poor train driver tried to stop. Going to their houses afterwards and telling their parents. Watching her father literally tear chunks of his own hair out with the grief.

There is so much in my head that I can't ever unsee.

Time has helped me to rationalise and to compartmentalise it all. Love and support along the way has helped me to heal, but back then my heart was broken, and I just couldn't cope with what I had seen.

I cried as I started to tell her about it all. There wasn't enough time to tell it all.

This was the real step towards change for me. Opening up and letting someone else see how damaged I really was. I'd been terrified of doing this and had held it back even from Sandra, the woman I loved.

There's catharsis in letting it out.

On with the process.

That session broke through the surface of my resistance. From then it became easier for me to speak about what I had seen and what I was feeling. I had a number of sessions with her where she heard a lot more about the incidents but mostly, we spoke about how I was travelling. I think that she realised early on that

I was broken and that I wasn't going to be able to get back on that horse.

The time moved along, and she recommended that I be referred to a panel of shrinks for assessment for medical discharge. They of course had to get second and third opinions so that meant a few sessions with two different psychologists and one psychiatrist.

I hadn't known before then what the difference was between those two professions.

Put simply, the psychologists try to analyse and help you through conversation and therapy. Psychiatrists take a more medical approach, and they try to use drugs to balance out your emotions.

But finally, after all of the assessments and poking around, the three experts all agreed that I had a good dose of PTSD along with depression and that I would not be able to return to work as a cop.

The time I spent with the various types of counsellors didn't cure me, but I started to change. In order to get through this process, I had to open up and show myself. It was forced change, and I did it then because I had to. Later on, I would find people who genuinely cared about me like Sandra, and I started to learn to open up to her and others about how I felt.

When I finally admitted to myself that I couldn't be a cop anymore. That was how I started to heal.

They medically retired me, and I had some breathing space to try to start again.

That meant finding a new job and working out how to function with all of the baggage I was carrying around. And here's where I need to talk a bit more about that baggage.

CHAPTER 9

Family Secrets

"I am not what happened to me. I am what I choose to become."

Carl Jung

I'M GOING TO TAKE a side journey that I need to talk about because I think the silence on this topic is something which needs to change. My silence also needed to change.

I've discussed how my time in the police service involved quite a few traumatic experiences. I thought I was dealing with them until the point where I realised that I wasn't.

There was one topic I never raised with the psychologist. I couldn't do it. I didn't think that it was relevant. I also kept it tucked away in the back of my mind, never allowing myself to be vulnerable enough to share it with anyone.

I was ashamed. I was frightened.

I'm telling it now because I should have faced it long ago. I needed to change in order to grow and move past it. I'm going to talk about it here because these secrets destroy lives.

Only later in my life did I realise that maybe a part of my inability to cope with the trauma in the police service possibly stemmed from the baggage I was carrying from childhood.

When I was four years old my grandfather raped me.

When I re-read that sentence, I can't really equate how life altering those ten words were for me.

Let's get it over and done with. Unfortunately, it's also a part of my story.

I'm an only child. My dad skipped out when I was about two years old. He popped in and out of my life until he died about ten years ago, but we didn't have a relationship worth speaking of. He wasn't a great guy, and my mum was probably way better off without him.

She didn't fare well on her own though, she never has.

After he left, mum and I lived in a unit in Southport on the Gold Coast. She would sleep in really late every morning, much later than three year old me. I later learned that was because of the Serapax (Valium) that she'd take every night.

In the mornings when I got hungry enough, I'd drag a chair over to the front door, climb up and open it. Then I'd get my bunny bowl off the bench and go and knock on our neighbours door. I can't remember her name, but she'd give me Weetbix, and I'd watch cartoons with her kids.

I think we stayed there for a while because I kind of remember that being a bit of a routine. I was very small, so my memories are hazy.

Mum ended up needing a bit more help and so when I was about four, we moved into the same set of units that my Nanna and grandad Bill lived in.

I remember that they were pretty actively involved with our day to day life. Mum was never a great cook, I joke that she's one of the few people I know who can burn water. That's not too far off the mark to be honest. Thankfully Nanna did most of the cooking.

The big social outing was for mum and Nanna to go play bingo. I remember going to a few day time games with them but once a week they'd go to the night time session, probably a Saturday night thing.

That was too late for me to go, it was past my bedtime. Bill would stay home and babysit me.

Sometimes mum would get me bathed and ready for bed before she left. Other times Bill got the added thrill of giving me my bath. That aspect was never threatening to me. As a kid you're an innocent right? A bath is a bath, and the adults wash you. I can't remember anything bad happening there but looking back through an adults eyes it makes my skin crawl.

Eventually I'd be put to bed. I remember so vividly how excited I was about my bed because although we were poor as anything, somehow mum or Nanna had managed to buy me Star Wars sheets and I was obsessed with them. Before the lights went out, I'd go through and name each of the characters. That was my nightly ritual.

Then I'd kneel beside the bed and say my prayers and then the lights would go out. We were all very good Catholics.

Somehow Bill must have been able to control himself during all of these processes.

It was only later, sometime after I'd gone to sleep that I'd wake up to have him roll me onto my stomach and pull my pyjama pants down. I remember that he would smell differently and I'm guessing that he must have had a drink or two before coming into the room. It didn't matter how much I screamed or cried, I'd feel his weight on me and the pain. The pain was terrible.

The most frightening part of it all was the suffocation. My face would be pushed into my pillow with his weight on me and I'd feel like I couldn't breathe. Even today I can't sleep with anything even slightly covering my face.

Then it would all stop, and he'd pick me up and take my bloodied pyjamas and sheets off and put them in the wash and tell me that I'd had a bad dream and had wet the bed.

And that's what he'd tell my mum.

Mum would tell me that I needed to stop wetting the bed, that I was a big boy. I was pretty ashamed of it.

Then one day I asked mum why when I wet the bed at night my pee was red. That led to some questions and I guess it all came out.

Well, it all blew up.

Lots of shouting and angry adults. Bill calling me a liar and yelling at my mum.

I didn't see Nanna and Bill for a while after that. Then one day mum sat me down and we had a long talk. She said that Bill had been very sick but that he had prayed to Jesus and that Jesus had made him better. She said that we could all be like Jesus and forgive him.

I didn't really know what to forgive him for. I was four and none of this made any sense to me at all.

And that was that. Happy families again although not long after that we moved away, and Bill didn't babysit me anymore.

Mum remarried when I was eight. Ron, my stepdad was a pretty good bloke. Very honest but very stern and not a great communicator. I got two older step-brothers, Geoff and Stephen as part of the deal.

Every second weekend we would go and stay with Nanna and Bill for the weekend. Everything seemed to be pretty normal.

When I was twelve Bill died. I hadn't really thought about all of this much until that point, but I must have been gaining some understanding because I remember being secretly kind of glad when I heard the news.

I don't know how my past impacted my teenage years. I went through what I thought was all of the normal teenage angst. I think that I really just kept the monsters locked away during that time.

At some point in my twenties, I connected with my Uncle Mick who had come out to visit us from Leicester, England. He was mums older brother.

Mum had told me many times that I was named after him. Mum had been six years old when Nanna and Bill brought her out with them from England to move to Australia. I knew that Uncle Mick had been twelve when they left, and he had stayed with his grandparents.

While Mick was over here, he told me his story. Bill had started abusing him and Uncle Mick had repeatedly run away from home to escape the abuse. Apparently, Bill had also built himself a bit of a reputation with some of the other local children and so Nanna and Bills migration to Australia was partially to get away from pretty nasty rumours. See, even here I find myself couching what should have been dealt with. Bill was a paedophile and had been abusing other children and so he and Nanna ran away to escape the allegations.

Uncle Mick had flat out refused to come and so Nanna had left him behind.

Here's the thing. I had long buried the memories of what had happened to me, but they were in a very shallow grave. And unfortunately for all of my life those bony fingers had been scratching through the soil every night in the form of night terrors and my fear of the dark.

I definitely remembered what had happened to me, I had just never really processed it.

Mum and I had to have a conversation.

We weren't very good at communicating with each other about anything real. She avoided conflict and most arguments were quickly quelled by avoiding the topic. We were really good at that.

I started the conversation by asking mum if she remembered Bill abusing me as a child. She quickly broke down and said she was so sorry it had happened.

What she said next is something that I've never been able to process.

Mum is very good at making anything into an issue about her. After a few minutes of telling me how sorry she was that it had happened she then tried to ally herself with me by telling me that it had happened to her too.

I was silent as she told me how ever since they left Uncle Mick behind Bill had turned his attention onto her, regularly raping her from age six into her late teens. She had rebelled as a teen and told Nanna about it and that had resulted in Nanna sending her off to boarding school as by then they had two other kids and didn't need a liar and a trouble-maker around.

Mum must have misread my silence for some kind of sympathy, and we left the conversation at that.

I couldn't, I still can't, believe that she had been victimised by Bill, but she still went out and left me alone with him.

I've never confronted mum about this.

The anger and rage I feel is counterbalanced by some kind of empathy for how she herself was victimised and called a liar. I've always seen her as being broken. I know what broke her and that could easily also have been me.

I can't believe that Nanna enabled Bill as much as she did. Her own son told her about him, but she chose to leave him behind rather than face Bill about it. Her own daughter told her about him, but she chose to put her in a boarding school rather than deal with it. Countless others made allegations which she ignored. All of that wilful blindness led to me being left in Bill's care.

Nanna too has long passed. On her death bed she said to me "Don't judge another person until you've walked a mile in their shoes." Yeah, it's a great quote and I do believe it. But not for this shit. The secrets that she kept have hurt so many. I know that Bill was the monster, but her silence enabled him. I've wondered so many times how different my life would have been if I had never experienced what Bill did to me.

Would I have been better able to cope with the Police Service if it had never happened? I'll never know.

I've written this very personal part about myself because I believe that it's relevant to change.

By speaking about it I'm creating change. No more secrets. It happened to me, and it has happened to others. I don't know if it ever happened to any other members of my family. None have spoken to me about it and frankly, they have their own stories to tell and their own lives to lead. I wish them all well.

But I believe that we force change when we stand up and hold people accountable.

I want others to gain the courage from my story to stand up and hold their attackers accountable. When we stay silent, we enable these people to find other victims.

My Nanna stayed silent, and she enabled Bill to abuse my mother. My mother was taught by Nanna to stay silent and that enabled Bill to abuse me.

I am not a victim.

We get to choose how we deal with our past. We get to choose how we act. We are who we choose to become. I'm me and I'm still standing. You might knock me down, but I will get up again.

I'm learning from others mistakes and I'm hoping that by telling my story it will help others to make these changes.

CHAPTER 10

How Do I Learn?

"Those that fail to learn from history, are doomed to repeat it."

Winston Churchill

I'VE TOLD YOU MY story about what led to me leaving the police service and the trauma behind it to illustrate just how much we can resist change when we are afraid. If I had known what my future after the police service looked like I would have leapt at the change. But when can we ever see the future?

Over the past seventeen years I've mentored and coached many small business owners. Through that work I've drawn heavily upon my own experiences to help them with their challenges. Along my journey I've found some amazing mentors who have helped me to re-examine my own experiences through an analytical lens.

We often learn subconsciously and change our behaviours or mindset without examining how we've done it. In learning how to coach others I've had to deconstruct my own experiences and learnings to understand how I myself have changed. Through that process I've found many tools to help me understand the learning process.

I always love the Conscious Competence Ladder tool developed by Noel Burch who was an employee with Gordon Training International. He states that when we learn a new skill, we step through four stages of competence. These are:

Unconsciously Incompetent   We don't know that we don't have this skill or that we need to learn it;

Consciously Incompetent   We realise that we don't have this skill;

Consciously Competent   We know that we have this skill;

Unconsciously Competent   We know that we have this skill, but we don't focus on it because it's so easy.

The best analogy I have for this model is in the context of learning to drive a car. As a child we sit in the back seat and watch our parents drive. They make it look easy so we believe that it's as simple as sitting there and turning the wheel. As children we're Unconsciously Incompetent, we'd be terrible drivers but we're completely unaware of how bad we'd be at it.

Then as teenagers we're given the opportunity to hop behind the wheel. Suddenly it all becomes real and we bunny hop down the road realising that this driving business is much harder than it looks. We become Consciously Incompetent.

Over time though, we gain confidence and skill and we pass our driving test. At that point we've gained competence in the skill but only marginally. We can drive but we're still (hopefully) cautious and very conscious of the steps that we need to follow, hence we're now Consciously Competent.

Fast forward to twenty years later when we arrive at a destination and can't recall how we got there. Driving is something that we're unconsciously competent at it. We don't think about how we do it, we simply do it on autopilot. We've gained mastery over that skill and are Unconsciously Competent.

I think about this model in the context of the life lessons I've learned and the opportunity I've had to analyse them.

Many changes that I have made in my approach to work, life and problems were made subconsciously, one could say in the unconsciously competent space. I simply got better at dealing with change and probably couldn't really articulate how I did it, I just did it. Does that make sense?

Having the opportunity to work with others and using my own experiences as frameworks enabled me to step back through that competency ladder. Because it's hard to teach something to someone else when you're unconsciously competent at it. Having the privilege of working with clients and having them share their personal challenges has helped me to look back at my own journey and to identify what I have learned within a conscious framework.

The first step in managing change in our lives is to ask ourselves how we do it?

Honesty can be difficult when we're looking internally.

What are our barriers? When do we resist? Are we continuing on because we're happy or because it's simply too hard to change?

CHAPTER 11

The Lesson

"Experience is a hard teacher because she gives the test first, the lesson afterward."

Vernon Law

WHEN I STARTED EXAMINING how I now cope more easily with change, I realised that I had been unconsciously working through a process. Examining the times when I had made changes in the past helped me to understand what was involved in that process.

Of course, for most of my life the changes I had made had been reactive. Which I guess is normal for most of us. A job sucks so we look for a new one. A relationship doesn't work out so we move on.

I think generally, we don't really think about how we do that. We just do it.

The problem is that reactive change may still mean that you're heading down the wrong path. I always think that decisions are better made when we run towards something, rather than when we are running away from something.

Think about that for a moment.

Most of us have either been the person or we know someone who has run from one toxic relationship only to end up in the next toxic relationship. Or we've quit a job we hate only to take another one which we'll hate just as much when the initial glamour wears off.

This is why I talk about conscious change. Working out where we want to go and running towards that goal.

To that end I started using a framework for change in my life. I call it the four C's. It helps me to understand where I sit within a situation or a problem and then what I need to do to move forward. The four C's are the stages of change. They are:

Catalyst, Courage, Change and Commitment.

A **Catalyst** is an event or situation which takes us to a cross-road. We can sometimes be in a situation for a long time before we hit that moment, that catalyst which forces us to make a change.

Courage is having the courage to make the change.

Change is when we act on our choice. That's when we put the wheels in motion to take that first step down one of the paths at the fork in the road. But to stay on that path we need Commitment.

Our **Commitment** is how we make the change stick. It's continuing to put one foot in front of the other on the pathway of our change.

Using that framework to see the reference points, let's look at my story.

Catalyst: For me, hitting rock bottom was my catalyst. It gave me enough of a reason to change. I'd known for ages that I wasn't coping, but nothing had taken me to the point of pushing me into acting. You've read my story and will have realised what I found in hindsight, that I should have acted long before I reached this point.

Courage: I had lacked the courage to make a change and so had reached a point where committing suicide seemed easier than quitting the police service and finding a new job. My moment in Stanthorpe gave me the courage to make the change that I needed to make.

Change: Sometimes the change can be simple, in my case it was handing in my resignation. That was one simple action which changed my course. Sometimes the change can be more complex, for example when we make a choice to get fitter. Then I see the change being when we join a gym, or we go for that first run.

Commitment: The fourth C is where most of us fall, the commitment. It's continuing to go to the gym, it's continuing to ease up on the drinking. For me it was about finding a way forward into a new job, a new career and building a sustainable life for myself. We need to have a plan on how we effect our change and to make sure that we have the capability to follow through with that plan. If we don't commit to it, then the other steps are pointless.

When we tell ourselves that we'll put up with a situation until X occurs we're just avoiding the issue. We have a catalyst but we're simply not brave enough to face it. The danger that we face is that when we kick that can down the road until eventually the situation can get worse, in my case Stanthorpe. Then we're forced to react, which means that we've lost control of the situation.

If I use the example of a relationship that you know is not working, but you just keep hanging in there until eventually it blows up, then you've lost control of that situation and your next steps will be reactive rather than conscious change.

So how do we shift to conscious change?

The first step is honesty. Honesty with ourselves.

If you know that there is something that needs changing in your life but you're just waiting for a catalyst then you've lost control of the situation. For example,

- If you've waited for a health problem before you start exercising or change your diet
- If you're waiting for a fight or an argument as an excuse to break up
- If you're waiting for a new job to pop up before you leave the job you hate

Then you're relying on an external catalyst to drive the change.

To make conscious change, we have to own the catalyst. Our desire for change is the catalyst. We take control again when we stop waiting to change and we step forward and make the change on our terms.

Let's talk a bit more about the barriers to change.

CHAPTER 12

Choice and Change

"It is our attitude toward events, not events themselves, which we can control. Nothing by is by its
own nature calamitous – even death is terrible only
if we fear it."

Epictetus

I WANT TO TALK FURTHER about why it was so hard for me to
accept that I needed to leave the QPS. I lost control of this
situation and so my reaction to the catalyst was almost fatal.

TJF, the job is fucked. I think that it was my third week on
the job when I first heard that phrase. I quickly learned that it
was the mantra of the Queensland Police Service.

For many it was a way of expressing their frustration at the handcuffs of bureaucracy, the legal system and the revolving doors of victims and criminals. I came to learn though that for others it was an expression of their lives. Trapped in a job they hated by mortgages, families, social expectations, and their own perceived lack of transferrable skills - "the job" slowly ate away at them and they gradually died inside.

Unless we're extremely fortunate in birth, most of us realise that we must work for a living. We go to school, we gain an education and skills and then we pursue a career path that we believe will provide us with financial success and happiness, often with less emphasis on the happiness part. I believe that most of us start our working life with optimism and enthusiasm for the future. I know that I really wanted to make a difference.

What happens when the enthusiasm dies? When the years start marching by and we find that we've lost our passion for what we do? What happens when the stress of your work is too much for you?

I believe that when this occurs that we have two choices. We can either change what we do, or we can change how we do it. I've personally experienced both types of changes and they're equally as hard.

It took me a long time to realise that I had to change what I did. I've written a lot above about the incidents leading up to my catalyst but long before that moment I think that I started to realise it the day that Dan walked out to the back of the station midway through his shift and shot himself. It was devastating.

That event hit home and was the starting point of me questioning whether I was in the right place.

Acceptance took longer. There was a huge stigma about being "too weak" or "a quitter". That's one of the reasons there are so many older, surly cops muttering TJF on a daily basis. Out of stubborn pride or perhaps fear of failure they never leave the job even though like me they have either experienced too much trauma or are just not psychologically suited for that role. They just stick it out and mask their problems with alcohol, depression, and failed relationships.

The same pushed me to the edge of my existence.

As it pushes so many others. As it has pushed so many others.

On the 20th of July 2023, while I've been writing this account, Senior Constable Kym Slade using her police issue firearm, took her life at Loganholme Police Station, my old police division. My old colleagues tell me that she was suffering from post-traumatic stress disorder, anxiety, and depression.

I can't speak about her individual journey. But every time I hear this familiar story, I think of how close I came.

Timothy J White has completed some interesting research into this within his thesis titled "Mateship, an enabling and protective factor associated with Queensland Police suicide" for James Cook University. The most troubling statistic from his research is that while the statistic on completed suicides amongst QPS officers is in line with the general populace, *the most alarming finding of this study was the higher rate of suicide attempts compared to the general population, where 1 in 10.5 officers report a history of a previous attempt, compared to the general population rate of 1 in 307."*

While that statistic makes me feel better about myself it also makes me incredibly sad.

Did all these other people feel as trapped as I did?

When I finally found the courage to make the change, my world changed. It wasn't an overnight change. For way too long I had agonised through indecision, fear of the unknown and fear that I wasn't good enough. But once I left and I found a new job and new pathways I eventually found happiness.

There is a lesson from my story that I can pass on to you. That lesson is that if you find yourself in a situation where you have lost all hope of finding enthusiasm and passion for what you do, then you must be brave enough to make a change.

Please don't run out after reading that and quit your job or your relationship. Before you take the nuclear option, it's worth exploring whether an internal change will make a difference.

Sometimes instead of changing what we do we can choose to change how we do it. Here's where I want to discuss how we find the pathways towards staying where we are but just doing it differently.

I now work with financial advisers, mostly the business owners or principals of their businesses. Over the past decade the financial advice profession in Australia has faced constant regulatory change, pervasive negative media attention and a huge increase in administrative burdens.

Many advisers I work with are finding it hard to keep their passion for helping their clients alive. It has been buried under mountains of compliance and administration.

I often get them to take some time away from the daily grind and to really think hard about what a good day at work feels like. What inspires them and makes them want to do more.

I did this exercise a long time ago and for me this has been about realising that my passion is helping people to be happy and to find satisfaction in what they do. That's my inspiration.

Once you've identified where your inspiration lies, try to find ways to spend more of your day doing just that. In my current work I regularly find that people are caught in their own behavioural patterns, holding on to the tasks that frustrate or stress them when it's possible to pass those along to others or to outsource them.

Be honest with yourself about what self-limiting behaviours you need to change. I've had many conversations with people who don't believe that they can change how they do what they do. When we change our mindsets and really start looking for solutions, we will often find them.

Can you bring back the fun and passion to a situation by doing things differently?

Try this exercise. Whether you're talking about your job or your life, take a moment in peace and quiet to write down what a perfect day looks like for you.

If it's your job, then what does a perfect day at work look like.

If it's your relationship, then what does a perfect day with your partner look like.

If it's your life, what does a perfect day in general look like for you.

Then, compare that with what it looks like now. What can you change to bridge that gap?

It might just be that you can change enough to make it work for you. Or it might be that the gap is just too great in which case a bigger change may be needed.

It's then about being brave enough to make that change.

CHAPTER 13

Courage

"And one has to understand that braveness is not the absence of fear but rather the strength to keep on going forward despite the fear."

Paulo Coelho

I'VE SPOKEN ABOUT KICKING the can down the road and hanging in there even when we know we should change. So what holds us back? Fear. The opposite of fear is courage, or is it?

What's the difference between fear and courage?

Master H, aged five once told me that he thought that one of his friends from school was brave because he wasn't afraid of the dark.

I thought carefully about this before replying. What I told him was.

To me, courage isn't about lacking fear. Courage is experiencing fear but not letting it stop you. Fear is what we feel, bravery is about how we choose to react to that feeling.

One of the bravest acts I have ever seen came from an unlikely source and it changed my perception of fear and bravery forever. That led in turn to my realisation about choice.

In my early twenties while working in the Cairns area I worked with cops of all shapes and sizes, both physically and mentally. We were regularly in physically confronting situations and different people approached these scraps with widely differing attitudes.

Some of the people I worked with loved a scrap and would take on any antagonist with enthusiasm. They were fearless and would always be front and centre in any situation that got out of hand.

Others would avoid physical confrontations as much as possible, often to their detriment as at the end of the day, we had a job to do.

One such was Jenny. Slight of build, in her late thirties Jenny had a quiet girlish voice and a very gentle disposition. She was a great person, fantastic with victims but amongst those of us tasked with training first year constables, she raised serious doubts about her reliability if our safety depended upon her.

That changed one night when Jenny and I encountered an angry mob from an out-of-control party.

A sixteen-year-old girls birthday party had been crashed by a group of adults in a rough neighbourhood in Cairns. Those people called in their friends, and it resulted in a large mob people fighting in the streets, overturning cars and smashing the neighbours houses.

Jenny and I arrived on our own but had to pull back when our car started being targeted by flying bricks and bottles. We called for back-up, but resources were light, so we received only one other unit with another two cops to help us bring the situation under control.

We pulled our two police wagons up a street away and locked our guns safely inside, they would have been useless, even dangerous to us as there was a high probability that we would be mobbed and have them taken from us. This was in a time before tasers and capsicum spray so apart from our guns we only had our police issued batons to rely upon.

Our plan was straightforward and highly risky. The four of us would walk down the middle of the street with our batons out and simply rush anyone who threw anything at us or committed any other offence in front of us. We'd then form up around that person and lock them in one of our wagons. We'd then repeat the process until the street was clear or we filled our two wagons.

I'd had had my share of bad days but to step forward at that point was inviting what could be termed a very rough day in the office. We knew that we were ridiculously outnumbered and that the chances of getting seriously injured were high. But we had a job to do, and this was one of those times when we had to step up to the plate, once you have that uniform on, you can't run away when innocent people are being hurt in front of you.

We walked together into the street, and it was chaos. We paused about fifty metres from the mob and my legs were jelly. Jenny, who weighed probably thirty kilos less than me had tears in her eyes as she said to me, "Mick, I'm really scared."

I grabbed her hand briefly and said, "Jen, we don't have a choice, this is what we signed up for."

That's when I saw it. She was absolutely terrified, but she stepped forward beside me and together we walked into hell.

She was afraid but she didn't let it stop her, she still chose to step forward.

I don't know how we pulled it off, but we did. By the time we got the street under control we were all bloody, bruised and battered. I'd had my shirt ripped off, Jen had a black eye and Rob had three broken ribs. In the process we had arrested sixteen people, and they were crammed into our two wagons. Getting the last few into each had been quite the challenge.

I was so bloody proud of Jen. Truth be told, I was proud of all of us.

That moment taught me a lot. Sure, I could work through my own experiences with fear but to witness that determination in someone else was so powerful. I saw first-hand that courage wasn't about being fearless. Bravery is about choosing to step forward even though your bowels are loose with fear and your body is shaking in terror.

Fear can take many forms. Personally, I've found that sometimes my psychological fears have been even more debilitating for me than the fear of physical danger.

The times when I've experienced:

- Fear of confrontation.
- Fear of change.
- Fear of admitting when I've screwed up.
- Fear of hurting someone else.

Fear can hold us back from being ourselves. The fears that control us can make us keep the job that we hate, stay in the relationship that we don't want, stop us from taking the risk of being hurt.

Don't get me wrong, fear has a purpose. Fear keeps us safe. It tells us that our actions can have consequences. Lacking fear is probably worse. Fearlessness is recklessness.

The balance is for us to control our fears rather than let them control us. Let the fear help you to assess the risk. Take the time to measure the depth of the water before you jump.

It's normal to be afraid. Stepping up when you're afraid is what makes us brave. That's the choice we can all make.

Regardless of what we feel, we can choose how we react to that feeling.

That's where I come back to bringing forward your choices and the changes you need to make. You can fear the unknown and the outcomes of your decisions, but you can't let that fear hold you back.

You can choose how you react to your fear. Then take a deep breath and take that step forward. Once you've done that, then you just need to commit to the change.

.

CHAPTER 14

Uncomfortable Conversations

"The most valuable of all education is the ability to make yourself do the thing you have to do, when it has to be done, whether you like it or not."

Aldous Huxley

I FEEL THAT THE MOST common overlap between courage and change lies in the area of having hard conversations. Throughout my own experience and also my experience with coaching others this is the space where courage seems to frequently elude us.

While some personality types have no issue at all with commencing a difficult conversation, the majority of us seem to struggle with it. One sad incident I encountered demonstrated how far we can go in avoiding those hard conversations.

I thought that after leaving the police service and entering the world of financial services that I had left the death and dying behind me. Sadly death is part of life and encroaches on every field, we can never run away from it. Several years ago I received the news that one of my clients had passed away. He was a sole operator and the sole director of the company he ran. I went out to see his family and to discuss with his wife what needed to be done to tidy up his business and sell it.

His family were obviously very upset as his passing was unexpected. When I sat with his widow, she told me that he had chosen to take his own life. She then read out to me parts of his suicide note. In that document he told her the things that he couldn't bring himself to tell her in person. He told her that his business was slowly losing revenue, that changes to the industry were too hard for him to keep up with and that he felt as though he was a failure.

As she read these things to me she told me that she had no idea. She had noticed small changes in his behaviour but he had given her no indication that he was struggling with the business or how he was feeling. She was calm, dignified and accepting of his choice but I could see how hurt she was that he hadn't been able to tell her what he was going through.

I think about her and how she would much have preferred to have had the hard conversation with her husband at the time than to lose him to his fear of opening up.

I've seen so many people in these situations. People unable to tell their partners about failures in their jobs or their businesses. People unable to speak up when they've made mistakes.

People who haven't found the courage to have those hard conversations.

And they are hard conversations. We know that the other person is going to react to our message, and for some of us the fear of those repercussions is probably much worse than the actual repercussions themselves.

These conversations can create change and that can be terrifying. It is the unknown. Your boss may fire you. Your business or relationship partner may leave you.

The most common difficult conversation most of my clients have procrastinated on over the past few years has been with underperforming staff members. I've seen people put these conversations off for years, justifying the procrastination through timing, capacity or any number of reasons. But always, behind it all knowing that it was going to happen eventually.

When we procrastinate on these hard conversations we're secretly hoping that the problem will disappear. That our job or our business will improve, that our employees will change their behaviours, that the person we want to break up with will break up with us instead.

Let's be honest. That's hope rather than action.

That's when we're waiting on that external catalyst rather than taking control of change.

The lesson I have learned for myself and through helping others is that finding tools to having difficult conversations can help us to find the courage to ending that procrastination. There are plenty of coaches or online resources out there designed to help us to structure and rehearse a hard conversation, enough so that I won't try to share all of their ideas here.

If you know that you have to have one of those conversations. Take the time to research, plan out and practice the delivery. Taking that positive step can help you to find the courage to make the change.

It still won't be easy but there's a common military adage that sums up preparing for it perfectly.

"Proper prior planning prevents piss poor performance."

If the thought of that conversation is causing you anxiety, please believe me that delaying it will not make it any easier. Yes, the conversation may be a catalyst for change. Yes, change and the unknown can be frightening. But living with fear and anxiety over the long term can be far worse than the temporary pain of a difficult conversation and its consequences. I can tell you that from my own personal experience.

CHAPTER 15

Commitment

"Our greatest weakness lies in giving up. The most certain way to succeed is always to try just one more time."

Thomas Edison

EARLIER I SPOKE ABOUT the four C's with the fourth being commitment. About how once you've made a change, sticking to that commitment is important. I'm going to tell a story here that haunts me and drives home to me exactly how important commitment is. We make changes for a reason. The catalysts we encounter and the choices we make drive those changes. However once removed from the situation it can be so easy to let our resolve waiver.

For a while when I worked in Cairns I specialised in Domestic Violence. This can be one of the most heart-breaking areas of police work. It's so easy to view criminals as the shady under-world type figures or as unintelligent thugs. When you work with DV you start to see what goes on behind closed doors in the suburbs. That monsters can be living right next to us, putting a smiling face on terror on a daily basis.

One particular case stands out for me. Kate.

Like the boy from the burning car, Kate haunts me.

I first met Kate when we attended her house after her part-ner Max broke her arm. Her neighbours had called us after they heard shouting and screaming coming from the house. They had told our phone operator that it happened a lot.

Kate was in her mid twenties, maybe a couple of years older than I was at the time and I could tell that she was pretty but that she was hiding that well. She was wearing her hair hanging forward so that it was hard to see the bruising on her face and she kept her head down, struggling to make eye contact.

She couldn't hide her broken arm from us.

Kate didn't want us to take any action against Max. That's pretty common, the abused know that their partner will only make their life harder for them if they tell anyone else what's been going on. Fortunately Queensland had very strict obliga-tions on police to take action if we suspected or saw evidence of domestic violence. Until that legislation changed most reported complaints of assault from domestic violence ended up being dropped after the charges were laid, because the abuser would intimidate their victims.

Kate also didn't want to go to the hospital but her arm was very obviously broken. We couldn't force her but we managed to convince her to go. We arranged an ambulance for Kate to get to the hospital, and we took Max into custody while we filed a temporary domestic violence protection order against him.

We also had to take Kate's young daughter Sophie into the hospital as Kate had no other family in Cairns.

Kate was upset and obviously terrified about what had happened. At first, she was really antagonistic towards us, and I could tell that she knew that Max was going to blame her for our intervention. She continuously denied that Max had hurt her.

I'd been dealing with many victims of domestic violence and so I remained patient and calm and eventually I started to get her to open up. Her story was only too common.

She had left her earlier boyfriend, Sophie's father, behind in Western Australia and moved to Cairns for a new start. He didn't want anything to do with Sophie, nor was he interested in paying child support and so Kate wanted a new life away from his abuse. She had no friends or family in Cairns when she arrived, so she'd taken a job working in Max's fish and chip shop.

Eventually she'd ended up dating Max, more through loneliness and trying to build a future for Sophie than any real affection for the guy.

It was fairly easy for Max to hold financial control over Kate, and she had readily accepted that power imbalance, particularly because Sophie was being well looked after. Then slowly the other aspects of control started to show. The process was insidious and before Kate had realised it, Max was controlling who she spoke with, what she wore and where she went.

Max was jealous of any perceived attention that Kate received from men. He would become enraged if male customers in the shop gave her any attention and that was what had sparked the argument that night. Max had accused Kate of flirting with one of the young male customers and started calling her a slut and a whore before he threw her against the wall, breaking her arm.

What I've given above is a quick summary of information that took several days for myself and Trish the local DV co-or-dinator to get out of Kate. Not only was she afraid of Max, but she was also alone, vulnerable and felt as though she had no alternatives. He had destroyed any self-confidence that she had.

Trish and I spent a lot of time with Kate helping her to realise that she wasn't alone and that she did have choices. Her fears were holding her back but there was one thing different about this incident that became the catalyst for her change. This time while abusing Kate Max had also turned his temper on Sophie for the first time. He hadn't physically assaulted Sophie but while Kate would endure his abuse stoically, she would do anything to protect her daughter.

Kate finally made her choice and decided to make a change. The Domestic Violence Protection Order was amended to include no contact from Max and Trish found emergency housing for Kate and Sophie.

I was proud of Kate for being brave enough to make these changes and this was one of those moments when I found great satisfaction in my work.

Now it came down to commitment.

Not long after this incident, I finished working in the area of Domestic Violence and started working back in General Duties, responding to whatever jobs our communications room would send us to.

A few months later I was working one evening when we received an urgent call about shots fired. We put on the lights and siren and started heading towards the address. Something started nagging at me, I knew that address from somewhere.

When we arrived, I realised that we were at Max's fish and chip shop. A few people were at the front as we ran up, ready for whatever had caused the shots fired call to come in.

We quickly realised that we were dealing with a suicide. In the front of the shop, the body of a male who I assumed was Max was sat against the wall. A shotgun was in his lap and it was obvious that he had put the shotgun into his mouth and pulled the trigger. The result had been catastrophic, and he had obviously died instantly. Fortunately, it was neither of our first encounter with shotgun injuries to the head, so we were prepared for the gruesomeness of the scene.

We started asking questions from the crowd out the front and a neighbour advised that he was the one who had called. He said that before the gunshot he had heard yelling and a woman screaming. My guts went cold with that knowledge.

I went inside the shop, past the counter and out into the back area.

That's where I found her.

I recognised Kate from her dress. She had few clothes as Max had never let her buy nice things. That day she was wearing a sun dress that I'd see her in before. That was the only way that I could have recognised her. He had killed her by holding her face down into the chip fryer.

I ran outside and was violently sick. I can never forget what I saw or how I felt. I was only twenty-two years old.

Over the coming days we pieced together the story. We found out that a few months after Kate had moved away from Max, she had bumped into him at the shops. Max had convinced her that he was sorry and that he had changed. That life would be different if she just came back to him.

Kate was still alone, she was vulnerable and she wanted to believe that he would change for her.

I've written earlier about what's involved for a police officer to prepare a sudden death report for the coroner. There was a third victim in this scenario and that was one of the most heart-breaking aspects of this.

I was the one who had to tell Sophie that both her mum and her "stepdad" were dead. We had to put her into the states care as there was nobody else to take her in. She was eleven when I had that conversation with her.

Having that conversation with an eleven-year-old girl was one of the hardest things I've ever done in my life.

Whenever I think about commitment to change, I think about this story. We make changes in our lives for reasons.

I wish that Kate had held firm to her commitment. I don't blame Kate. I blame myself. I wish that I had spent more time with Kate to help support her in her commitment. I wish that I had helped her to find others to support her in her commitment.

That's the lesson I learned. That sometimes we need help from others to support us when we make a commitment to change.

Stay strong to your Commitments. Find those who will support you and lean on them.

For me, Kate is always one of those cases where I'll doubt myself. Could I have done more to support Kate? I don't think that I could have but I'll never forget her. Whenever my resolve waivers on an issue I remember Kate.

CHAPTER 16

Change and Growth

"Growth requires us to leave something behind. It can be habits, careers, beliefs, even people. Make space for grief in the process of growth. You have to mourn your former life to make room for a newer you."

Minaa B.

Y OU'VE CHANGED. EVER HEARD that before?
I've heard it a few times over the years. Sometimes it's hurt me badly. When I think back upon my life I can see many changes that I've made, either consciously or unconsciously. Some of those changes have cost me dearly.

Joining the police service was one of the first times that I heard it. The area I grew up in was pretty rough. As a teenager I don't think that I was a bad kid, but I had a lot of "friends" who had drawn the attention of the law on a few occasions. When I was eleven I'd been drawn into shoplifting chocolate bars from the local corner shop with my mates. Of course, first time I had a go at it I'd been caught and hauled home by the cops. The literal arse whipping that my stepfather gave me created a healthy fear of crossing the line from then on.

Still, on into my late teens many of my mates were pretty rough. There were a lot of drugs and many of them had some anti-social tendencies.

When I told the guys I hung out with that I was applying for the police service many of them gave me a lot of flak for it. "You'll become a dog." "Everyone will hate you." Just the usual kind of encouragement that you get from those who've broken the law a few times themselves. Nothing really changed at first because I don't think that many of them thought that I'd get in.

Then I surprised them all and got accepted into the academy. I've spoken before about how it immediately changed my perspective. I mentioned earlier that for the first time in my life I felt a collegial experience. I was now a part of something bigger. It was heady and exciting, a whole new frontier for me.

One weekend I reached out to one of my old mates and asked if he wanted to catch up. It was a flat no. He smoked a lot of pot and while that was never my thing I'd never been bothered by it. However he didn't want a bar of me now that I was training to be a cop.

I'd been so busy that I hadn't realised that those guys were avoiding me. I was still only young and somehow had not considered that my career choice would create such a distance between myself and them. I thought that we would remain friends. It was that moment that made me realise that my two lives were incompatible with each other. I learned then that I had to step away from them in order to keep going forward. The realisation hurt but fortunately my training demanded one hundred percent of my attention, so the sting was only momentary. I moved forward with purpose.

Funnily enough the reverse happened as I exited the QPS. Because I was leaving with the stigma of mental health issues, my circle of "friends" dropped very quickly. I've already written about that part earlier. That time it hurt a lot more.

These were the times when career changes impacted my personal relationships and I felt as though I had left people behind. In both of these cases I would have kept those relationships going but hindsight tells me that they weren't worth that effort. The people who mattered stuck with me and those who didn't weren't who I thought they were at the time.

There have been other times when my own personal growth has changed my relationships with others.

I was raised in a very white, Christian community. Queensland, Australia in the 70's and 80's and even through to today in some areas has been traditionally very racist and homophobic. While growing up I had very little contact with any other ethnicities and nobody was openly queer. Our language was full of terms for various minorities and the worst insults we could land on another boy was to call them a poof or fag.

Joining the Queensland Police Service in the early 90's didn't help to change those views. The QPS had corporate policies that focused upon inclusion but on the ground and on the streets we were a very bigoted group of people. If you had told me that while I was in the job I would have denied it vehemently. That's the nature of an indoctrinated bias. We can't see it because it's become interwoven with our personality and often it's echoed all around us by people who share the same beliefs.

Yes, you can be a good person with great intentions but still be a bigot. Until you deal with those ingrained prejudices that will remain the case.

Since leaving the QPS I have travelled a lot. I have worked with people of every race, religion and gender identity. Still, change didn't come quickly or easily. I carried my prejudices for a long time, until I started to learn individuals stories and how they had been treated differently because of who they were. Self-reflection told me that I too had treated people differently in the past.

While I can take some pride in having never been maliciously racist or homophobic, I'm saddened when I think of my ignorant acts and words from the past. Stupid, petty but horrible things when looked at through a lens of self-awareness. These aren't proud memories.

I think that all of us spend part of our lives trying to change whatever indoctrination we were given as a child. I know I've been unwinding my prejudices for many years now and still surprise myself when I realise another unconscious bias has surfaced. Now, for me it's about conscious and directed change towards an end goal of treating all people equally.

That growth has cost me relationships. I read somewhere that when we grow and change, our growth holds up a mirror to those around us who aren't prepared to grow, and that our changes highlight their own stagnation. That can cause friction in any relationship.

In this case my growth has been in my own values and the way that I treat other people. That change has been a difficult road to navigate. We don't want the people who we love and who have supported us to ever feel like they have been left behind. But we also have to choose how much we will sacrifice ourselves, our worth or our own personal growth for anyone else. I don't have the answers to this as every person's journey will be very different.

What I believe is that we must ask ourselves how much we value those people in our lives. When we reach moments of incompatibility in some areas, we have to determine whether those aspects are showstoppers or do we value enough of our remaining compatibility to continue on with the relationship.

Sometimes we have to have the hard conversation and know when to move on. We will grieve when that happens, but there are times when it's the only way for us to find our own true worth and happiness.

I've learned through those heartaches to surround myself with the people who will not only support my own growth but who will challenge and encourage me to grow. I'm sad about the people who are no longer a part of my life but I'm also a realist enough to know that the divides between us are too far for those relationships to remain.

If I'm honest, when I grieve those relationships I'm missing the past, not something that would endure the future.

To me our resilience through these changes comes back to those four words. Insistence, Persistence, Resistance and Consistence. Insist on putting your values first, don't ever compromise on them. Be persistent in wanting to grow, it's the nature of every living thing to evolve and grow with time. Resist the urge to let comfortability and familiarity keep you from growing. Finally, be consistent in your efforts to be more tomorrow than you are today.

If you can stick with that formula, you will know when you have to step forward, be brave and leave your past behind – even when it hurts like hell to do so.

CHAPTER 17

Owning Change

"If you don't like something, change it. If you can't change it, change your attitude."

Maya Angelou

To me resilience and change are interlinked. As we deal with change we have to maintain our resilience to cope with the stresses that change puts upon us. I see it in the same way that we experience physiological changes when we work out physically. Whether it's on the treadmill, lifting weights or in the pool, those exercises stress our joints, tendons and muscles, creating tears and discomfort. If we push through that discomfort we then start to see change and growth.

I've spoken about some of my personal experiences with moving towards conscious, intentional change. Let's recap and summarise what I have learned along the way.

Time to Stand Up

I'm standing up and talking about how I fell and how I considered suicide. It can be a taboo topic, one which many people are uncomfortable talking about but I see gradual change happening in society. I've chosen to make my story public so that others can hear of my struggles and know that they're not alone, and that hopefully they can see that I managed to get through those times.

Some bad shit happened to me as a kid because secrets were kept. I'm standing up, telling my story and hoping to continue to make change in our society in stopping these types of secrets from destroying people's lives. While writing this book and sharing the draft with a close long term friend, he opened up about similar things which happened to him. Things that he's never shared with another adult but which have haunted him throughout his life. I was humbled that he shared his story with me but grateful that I could be there for him.

My message is to stand up and make change where you believe that it is important.

The Elements of Change

I've found my way of identifying change through the four C's. Catalyst, Courage, Change and Commitment. My story of hitting rock bottom is a perfect illustration of why we should never let our situation get that bad that our catalyst is catastrophic. There were plenty of other catalysts for change along the way for me but I was just not courageous enough at the time to take them.

Once you have found your courage then it's a matter of making the change. However big or small it may be. Then depending upon the nature of the change, finding the commitment to stick with it.

On Courage

Courage isn't about the absence of fear, it's about overcoming fear. Change can be frightening, the unknown can be terrifying. But, teaching ourselves to step forward when we feel that fear is liberating.

I've written about uncomfortable conversations and the courage we need to muster to have these conversations. You can try to avoid the uncomfortable conversations in life but then that will always mean that you are the one denying yourself happiness and fulfilment. In order to be true to ourselves we sometimes need to dig deep and have those difficult conversations, even when we know that the outcome is going to be messy and chaotic.

All we can do is prepare ourselves as best we can before we have those conversations, to make sure that we give ourselves the best possible chance of impacting the change afterwards.

On Commitment

Have you ever broken up with someone but then returned to them and regretted it? Have you ever started exercising and then given up? Have you ever given up a habit or addiction only to backslide. It's all about the commitment.

Lean on your friends, lean on your family, seek out whatever support you need to help you to stick with your commitments.

On Growth

It's only human for us to continue to grow and change as we get older. I'm very different at fifty to who I was when I was forty and a million miles away from who I was when I was twenty.

That change and growth has been through my own experiences, through choices I have made and from learnings I have taken from others. For me personally, that growth has involved changes in my value systems, in how I interact and view others by challenging the stereotypes and bigotry I learned as a child and a young person.

I've learned that through changes both externally via career choices and internally through personal growth that my relationships with others have sometimes changed over time. That there have been relationships which have endured as I have grown and there have been those who I've left behind when we simply lost our sense of commonality.

Find your tribe. Find the people who will support and challenge you to be who you need to be. Not change for the sake of change, but the change and growth that fills your soul and lets you be the person you really want yourself to be.

What Can You Do

Change is inevitable. Throughout our lifetime, our bodies will constantly change and with those physiological changes will come psychological changes. We're programmed through our very DNA to grow up then grow old and that process includes our mental faculties.

External stimuli will constantly force change around us as society adapts to innovation and socio-political upheaval. Internally we will (or at least we should) change in response to our own personal experiences and learnings.

My point is, go back to the model of Conscious Competence and make your changes consciously. Choose who you want to be and what's important to you, then work towards making positive changes in your life. Surround yourself with the people who will help you to grow and change.

When you're faced with change or the need to change. Dig deep and find the courage to own that change.

You can do it. If I can then I'm sure that you can too.

PART 3

We Get to Choose Our Mindset

I think that each of us is just a child wearing an
overcoat that we call adulthood. That coat is
made up of mortgages, jobs, and responsibilities.
It's up to us to be brave enough to
open that coat and let the child in us
be able to breath, play and live.

CHAPTER 18

In An Instant

"Life changes fast. Life changes in the instant. You sit down to dinner and life as you know it ends."

Joan Didion

O NE OF THE GREATEST gifts that my time in the job gave me was to experience things that would change my entire outlook on life. One of those is also one of the saddest stories I encountered.

This happened very early on in my career, about a week after Dan and I had lost the drowning victim at Trinity Beach, so I was still in my third month out of the Academy.

I was working on a morning shift, starting at six am in general duties. Franko and I were handed our first job before we even left the station, a sudden death in Smithfield, Cairns. We arrived at a house in the middle of suburbia and were met at the front door by a very upset young girl, she was around sixteen and looked like she had had a hard night.

She took us through the house into the bathroom and there, slumped in the shower was her best friend, Anna. I checked her vitals, and she not only didn't have a pulse, but her skin was cool to the touch, she'd been dead for a few hours.

It was such a depressingly sad scene, and I felt such pity. Anna was a strikingly pretty girl, sixteen years old and while we were both professional, it felt so wrong to see her naked and vulnerable like this. Nobody should ever see another human lose their dignity in this way.

The story of how she came to die in the shower was even sadder. Jill, her friend had invited Anna over for the night because Jill's parents were away. The two girls had invited a couple of older boys over and they had all had quite a bit to drink together. Anna had had a real crush on her guy for quite a while and so after a few drinks they had slept together and that had been the moment when Anna had lost her virginity. Apparently after they'd had sex, she had asked this guy whether they were in a relationship now and he had laughed at her and left.

This had apparently broken Anna's heart. She was drunk, vulnerable and made some bad decisions.

One moment which changed not just her life but that of many others.

Anna had gone through the bathroom cabinets and swallowed every pill that she could find, washing them down with more vodka.

Jill told us that her boyfriend had left and that's when she came out and found Anna throwing up. She hadn't realised that Anna had taken the pills and had just assumed that she'd drank too much. She had put Anna in the shower and helped her clean herself up. She said that Anna had stopped throwing up and had pushed her away, telling her to leave her alone and just sat in the shower, crying.

Jill had then gone into the living room and passed out on a couch. She said that she'd woken up hours later and realised that the shower was still running. She'd checked on Anna and realised that she was dead. That's when she called for an ambulance.

She was inconsolable, hungover and in extreme shock.

We managed to find where Jill's parents were and got them to come home. We waited for them to arrive before we left because there was no way that we could leave Jill on her own.

In the meantime, we'd arranged for the wagon to come and collect Anna. We had to help them and while I've seen many dead bodies in many gruesome situations, I felt so uncomfortable having to pull this naked young girls body out of the shower. I was just one year older than the guy she had slept with the night before and my heart ached for her dignity.

Franko and I slowly drove around to Anna's address and on the way, Franko told me that this was my job. I had never delivered a death message before. I felt sick to my stomach.

When we arrived at Anna's house, I could see that it was just a normal house in the middle of suburbia. I remember thinking that it was all so surreal.

We parked out the front and I looked at the time, it was 7.30am in the morning. After lots of deep breaths and with some reassurance from Franko, I got out of the car, and we walked towards the front door.

From the front path we could see into the dining room. Three people were sitting on bench stools eating what look like cereal. I assumed that they were Anna's mother, father and younger brother. They looked like any normal family enjoying a normal Saturday morning together.

And I was about to fuck up their lives forever.

It hit me like a punch to the gut, the feeling at that moment was so visceral. When I knocked on that door and told them this news their normal happy life was going to change direction forever.

I knew that I couldn't change what had happened. That was out of my control. But I wanted them to have every extra minute that they could of normality, of happiness. And I sure as hell didn't want to be the one that stole that happiness from them.

That's when I realised how short life was and how we can't take any day for granted. We need to live each day as though it could be our last.

People say shit like that all the time and it can feel hollow. For me, that moment I realised exactly how real that perspective needs to be. We just don't know what's around the corner. Anna in a drunken silly moment ended her story. But in that moment, she inexorably changed the path of so many people around her.

I was holding back the vomit when I knocked on the door. Her dad answered us, and I could see the confusion and sudden fear in his eyes when I asked if we could come in and speak with them. When two cops knock on your door and they're holding their hats in their hands, you know it's going to be bad, right? But still people can never believe how bad it will be.

Somehow, stammering and crying myself, I gave them the news. I did it many times again over the years and it never got any easier. Sickeningly terrifying.

Like most people, they couldn't really comprehend the news at first. People go through immediate denial. There must be a mistake, it can't be our daughter.

We had been taught at the academy not to couch these messages. Human nature wants to soften the blow, to say that a person has passed, moved on, ended their suffering, gone to a better place.

We couldn't couch it. Because this news is always so traumatic any form of couching it will cause people to think that there's still hope. As hateful as it is. We had to destroy all hope. We had to use the words "She is dead."

I learned then to watch the various stages of denial and comprehension in people's faces.

Then there was that moment when they realised it was true. Seeing another human break at that point is unbearable. I give all of my love and support to the cops, nurses and doctors out there who still do this today. It's fucked.

Remembering them both in that moment still breaks my heart. Her little brother still couldn't quite grasp it but for her mum and dad, that moment was agonising.

That day changed the way that I live my life forever and I will never forget it. I am grateful for every day that I have. I try to live it like it could be my last.

I'm told that I always appear happy. I'm glad that people see that in me because that's how I want to be. There's a reason for it.

This. The realisation that the course of our lives can change in an instant so extract every bit of joy that you can, while you can.

I try to do that. I try to be happy and to make the people around me happy.

Every day of my life.

CHAPTER 19

Full Moon

"Hoping for the best, prepared for the worst, and unsurprised by anything in between."

Maya Angelou

T HROUGHOUT THE COURSE OF this book, I'm talking about different incidents and how they have impacted me and what I have learned. Some gave me some profound lessons, others gave me nightmares.

There's one which left me with so many questions but taught me more about paying attention to the people around us.

I'm always wary about the full moon. People do crazy things under a full moon.

It might sound like a superstition, but some of the weirdest stuff I've ever seen happened during those times. The sad part is, that sometimes people will make those split second decisions then which can change lives.

One such really sticks in my memory.

We were working a midnight to eight am, the dreaded nightshift in Cairns. The good thing about our rostering system then is that they'd roster us for seven of these in a row and then when we finished on the last Wednesday morning, they would normally roster our days off straight after. And the whole station ran on this system so there'd usually be a group of twenty or so of us finishing on the same day. It would be an eight am finish on the Wednesday, we'd all go out for "Nightwork Breakfast" which meant that a local pub would open up and let us get on the sauce at 8.30am and hopefully sometime later that day (sometimes that evening) we'd get home and have another four days off in a row.

And doing a few in a row meant that by night three you were in a bit of a routine.

On one of these occasions, my partner and I got called to a shooting at about three am in the morning. It was out the back of nowhere and apparently a young bloke had run to a house, telling the occupants that his mate had been shot out in the bush.

We drove to that house and picked up this young lad. Funny how that's what I thought of him when he was eighteen and I was about twenty-one at the time. He told us that he and his mates were parked up in a spot a couple of kilometres away, so we put him in the back and drove through the bush trails until we found the spot.

It wasn't a great scene.

Five mates had driven out into the bush to have a few drinks around a campfire and fuck around as only young blokes on the piss will do.

His mate Brendan had been in great spirits, no signs of depression, just a young bloke having fun with his mates and drinking too much beer and rum.

Until he pulled out the shotgun and shot himself.

Before we go any further, I'll talk a bit about suicide.

It's normally a solitary thing. I've seen one person who had self-immolated, that is they walked into a petrol station, poured petrol all over themselves and lit themself on fire. They apparently did that to make a point to their ex. I've seen a couple that have lain down over train tracks, including a couple of young teenagers who did it together in a very tragic double suicide. But rarely will someone commit suicide while around a group of friends.

I believe that this was a bit of "fun" that went too far. Apparently, Brendan had pulled out the shotgun and been joking around about it, one of the other guys told him to be careful with it so he had propped it under his chin and laughed as he pulled the trigger.

I would like to believe that he was drunk and thought that it wasn't loaded.

It was loaded and it had split his head apart like only a shotgun blast at close range can do.

His mates were in shock and terrified. In these circumstances we had to treat this as a suspicious death which meant that we had to preserve the scene for the Scenes of Crime and Detectives to come out. The boys had loaded Brendan onto the back of their Ute and that's where he lay, half propped up.

After a quick conversation, Harmsy, my partner as the senior man said that he'd put the other boys into our car and drive them into the station to be interviewed and organise for the others to come out and start investigating.

My job was to sit in the middle of the bush, under the full moon, with Brendan's body until they came.

We were at least an hour's drive from Cairns station where the SOC and CIB worked and we had no radio contact where we were, so I knew that I was probably looking at around two hours out at the scene.

Did I mention earlier that while I have plenty of experience with them, I'm still scared of dead bodies?

I found myself facing a dilemma. I could sit by the campfire with my back to the bush and the darkness and face Brendan's headless body on the back of the Ute.

I could sit with his body behind me, facing out into the darkness and the sounds of the bush.

Instead, I opted to stay walking around the area, keeping a wary eye on Brendan while also keeping an eye on the bush.

While I have nightmares, I'm never afraid to be outside in the dark. I can walk through the night without a torch without feeling scared but in that situation, I was terrified. The situation itself was bad enough but seeing the bush and the scene under the full moon just gave me the heebie jeebies. I jumped at every noise, and I kept on swinging my torch around into the shadows, while checking to make sure that Brendan hadn't in fact moved while my back was turned.

It seemed like forever until I saw headlights coming towards me through the bush and I've never been so relieved to see those cars come in.

The investigation into Brendan's death ended up being summarised as death by misadventure. There were no indications of depression or mental illness, just a young bloke trying to be funny and making a horrible mistake. But we'll never know.

Each of his mates who were present that night, along with his mother and father and other family members, will always question whether they missed something, some clue along the way of whether there was something that drove that decision.

I learned a lesson that day about the people I care about.

Make sure that you pay attention to them.

I get told sometimes that I give big squishy hugs. There's a reason why. I think it's important to let people know that you care. I will grab the people I care about and hug them close to me and then hold them and look into their eyes. I try to really see them, to not take them for granted and to let them know that I'm always there for them.

And that's what I learned from this incident, to hold your loved ones tight.

CHAPTER 20

Make Every Moment Count

"Life changes on a dime, so live life to the fullest."

Max Holloway

IT'S SO EASY TO take things for granted. We have so many moments in our life that we allow to slip by because we're distracted, we're on our phones, we're simply not present. I want to share a story that I use to remind myself to make the moment count. To be present and to appreciate how wonderful every moment can be.

Once a year in Far North Queensland, all the local Pony Clubs converge on the small town of Ravenshoe for the Ravenshoe pony club camp. A long weekend of all horse related activities with the main event being the Ravenshoe cross country course.

Ravenshoe is a beautiful town on the Atherton Tablelands about three hours west of Cairns. It's famous for being the town at the highest altitude in Queensland and so in winter it's cold and wet. Perfect conditions for a long weekend of camping with horses.

At that time, I was one of the senior riding instructors for the region and so I would volunteer my time over the weekend to help organise the event and to supervise the cross-country course. That wasn't an honour, the cross-country course was a death trap and every year there would be several broken bones as kids and adults would try to convince their ponies and horses to jump over such fun obstacles as picnic tables and overturned boats. It was my first time being saddled with the job and so at age twenty-two I was nervous about the responsibility.

I was engaged at the time to a girl named Jodie. She was a beautiful girl who I'd met a couple of years earlier when she was eighteen and I was twenty. She'd approached me about getting riding lessons and well, we fell for each other. She was competing over the weekend, but I wasn't worried about her. She was a natural rider and could face any of the challenges.

Somehow, we got through the Friday and the Saturday with only a broken collar bone from one of the adults and a fractured wrist from one of the kids. By all reports one of the most successful first two days of the camp in recent memory. I wasn't so sure about that as I'd had to be the one to give first aid in each case. The fact that I was a cop meant that myself and Donna Chaplain, the local nurse got all the bandage duties.

Sunday would be our last day and so Saturday night was always a night for everyone to have a bit of fun. It was bloody cold up there and so we'd made a fire and pulled our camp chairs close while we had a drink and a laugh.

Jodie and the other ladies all retired but to their dissatisfaction, a group of four of us blokes were comfy and happy by the fire with our rum and cokes in hand.

It was me, Donna the nurses son Mark and two of the old pony club dads, believe it or not Bob and Dave.

We sat around that fire for hours, the rum keeping us warm and the laughter coming easily as we told jokes and stories to each other. It was a full moon, and the air was so crisp and still that it was perfect. At one point or another each of the four of us remarked on how it was a perfect night.

Mark was the local butcher. He was twenty-three and a real larrikin. He was quick to laugh but if someone pissed him off, he'd throw hands just as quickly. Then after a dust up he'd shake the other bloke's hand and buy him a beer. He was a big lad, around six foot three and over one twenty kilos and he and I were a pair because we both rode the two biggest horses in the area. He had a rangy older chestnut thoroughbred called Struth and I'd brought Bear up for the weekend, my seven-year-old Holsteiner cross thoroughbred. Both horses were close to eighteen hands tall, and both were given a wide berth by everyone else because they were a couple of mean pricks. Bear was a right bastard for biting and Struth liked to let a hoof fly from time to time. Mark and I had hit if off right away because we were the only ones who could ride each other's horses. Bear had thrown three of the other instructors in one day much to Marks and my delight and Struth had a similar record. We both loved our horses and were happy to find a fellow who could ride each other's unrideable bastards. It wasn't that we were great riders, we both just were comfortable with these cranky giants.

Back to the night at hand.

Our laughter continued as the night went on, as we all shared stories and told yarns. The two old blokes had been around and had some whoppers to share and Mark's laughter would boom out from time to time prompting Jodie and the other ladies to poke their heads out of the tents and tell us to keep it down.

Suddenly Dave gave a howl of pain and started dancing around. He was swatting his leg and yelling that something had bitten him. We of course offered our support, in spirit anyway, because the sight of him doing a jig around the fire slapping himself with his worn out Akubra hat had us in stitches. We were useless to help him and the more he howled about it the harder we laughed. Mark of course being the loudest amongst us with tears rolling down his ruddy cheeks.

There are some nasty ant species up through the tablelands and we all suspected that's what had bitten Dave. Their bites can be bloody painful, but we did what all good friends do and helped him through it by laughing at him.

We were all just starting to settle down when it was Mark's turn to get bitten. He jumped up screaming "It's got my ballsack!"

I'll never forget it.

He was a big bloke and so when he started thrashing around trying to cup his balls and get the ant out of his pants, it was pandemonium. Camp chairs were knocked over and drinks went flying. He pulled his jeans down to his knees and had his hand in his jocks trying to get the bastard ant off his balls.

Bob, Dave, and I were useless. Bob and I had fallen off our chairs laughing so hard and trying to get out of the way of Mark's windmill. Dave was only just starting to come good from his bite, so he was gleefully jumping around yelling "I fucking told you they hurt! Sucked in ya useless bastard – serves ya right for laughing at me."

I joke about laughing so hard that you get snot bubbles, well this was one of those times. I will always remember laughing so hard that night that I thought I'd broken a rib. Tears rolling down my face, jaw aching and the knowledge, even then that it was something special. As I crawled into the swag with Jodie, I remember telling her that it was a night I would remember forever.

A week later Mark was dead.

I try to remember him from that night, not how I saw him next.

He was at work boning out a hanging forequarter and on a downward stroke his knife slipped off a bone and the force of it swung his arm down so that his boning knife embedded itself in his upper thigh, nicking the femoral artery.

The Ravenshoe ambulance was out of town so the girl on the counter of the butcher's shop rang his mum Donna at the doctor's surgery she worked at five hundred metres away. Donna ran down to him and tried to staunch the bleeding on the sidewalk outside the butchers while they waited for the ambulance to arrive. He bled out in her arms there and was gone by the time the ambulance got back into town.

The word spread over the next couple of days throughout the community and it hit me like a punch to the guts. Bill was the closest relative who'd passed and who gave a fuck about him. I hadn't lost any friends or anybody I personally cared about before. That night had sung to me, and Mark had been larger than life and for him to suddenly be gone was such a shock.

And Donna, poor Donna. I couldn't believe it.

Most people don't realise it but unless you have a pre-existing medical condition which your treating doctor will certify as the cause of death then every death must have a post-mortem examination so that the police can prepare a report for the coroner. Even an accident like Mark's where the cause of death is obvious starts a process where the medical examiner accompanied by a police officer literally pulls the corpse apart to examine the brain and internal organs, take samples of tissues and fluids and test for various drugs and poisons. It's a very invasive process where the organs and brain are all removed, weighed, and sliced open for tissue samples. In Cairns at that time this was all done with the police officer being hands on, picking up the organs handed to them by the medical examiner and weighing them and recording the details so that we could prepare the report.

That was my job at the time.

The next time I saw my friend was on the slab. Kennedy the medical examiner spared me as much as he could, but I still had a job to do and had to observe the process.

I had to dig deep and keep my thoughts distant and removed while I did my job but in the back of my head I was screaming at the injustice and indignity of seeing my friends body dissected and his secrets laid out on the stainless-steel bench.

I'd seen it all before and was no longer squeamish, the process can be quite interesting but not this time.

The scream of the bone saw as Kennedy cut through Marks skull drove needles through my brain. Watching his gloved hands reach into the skull cavity and sever the brainstem and carry my friend's brain over to the scales, sitting it beside his heart and his liver, was a vision I've tried to wash from my mind for many years.

I try hard to remember him by the fire that night and to think that what I saw in the morgue at Cairns Base Hospital was just a shell.

That night in Ravenshoe was a perfect moment and I'm so lucky that I didn't let it pass me by. I regularly remind myself of this story to remind myself to pay attention to where I am and who I'm with, because you never know when that perfect moment may arise that you will need to hold with you for the rest of your life.

Try to be present. Don't let these moments pass you by.

CHAPTER 21

My Theory of Relativity

"I've learned that people will forget what you said,
people will forget what you did, but people will never
forget how you made them feel."

Maya Angelou

I SAW A MEME RECENTLY which read "Someone who drowns in 7 feet of water is just as dead as someone who drowns in 70 feet of water. Stop comparing traumas, stop belittling your or anyone else's trauma because it wasn't 'as bad' someone else's. This isn't a competition, we all deserve support and recovery."

I can't attribute the original source to this but it rings true for me. Each of us has our own story. I've told part of mine here. You will have your own story to tell.

Your journey will be relative to you. Seen through your eyes and felt through your feelings.

What I can say is that I have often been my own worst critic. In the past I have minimalised my own feelings, telling myself that I was weak or a loser for being overwhelmed by my experiences. Others had faced so much more than me and found their way through, who was I to complain? That was part of my reluctance to leave the police service. That other cops were doing just fine, so why couldn't I just toughen up?

I wish that someone had told me not to compare. I wish that someone had told me that we all have our own challenges to face. I wish that someone had told me to be kinder to myself.

You're reading this so I have the opportunity to say it to you.

What breaks me may be just an average day for you and vice versa. We all have our own strengths and weaknesses. Don't compare your life with anyone else's. Don't judge yourself against any other person.

Be yourself.

Be kind to yourself. Be kind to others. Learn from others. Be curious and learn about their lives.

When someone tells you about challenges they have faced, ask them what they learned. Ask them what they would do differently. Ask them what they're proud of.

It's not about what we face, it's about how we face it.

You'll get knocked down, but you can get up again.

To me that's the mindset of success.

CHAPTER 22

My Choice

"Nothing is more beautiful than the smile that has struggled through the tears."

Demi Lovato

THROUGHOUT THE PRECEDING PAGES I've spoken about building resilience, owning change and choosing our mindset.

In writing the contents of this book I've had the opportunity to reflect upon my own journey, the challenges I've faced and the lessons which I have learned. I can't change the past but I can learn from it. I chose my mindset long ago.

I've chosen to react with happiness. I've chosen to live a life that counts and one that I am content with. So here's my summary for you.

Stand UP!

While I've heard many others stories, I have only my own experiences to truly know how my childhood abuse impacted me. I will say that as a man I felt great shame in what happened to me and I guess like many other men, I wanted to hide my shame from the world. It's taken me many years to realise that there is no shame. I did nothing wrong. The man who did this and the people who kept his secrets are the ones who carry the shame. I hold my head high now, thanks to the love and support of people who reminded me of this.

But there is something that I'm going to ask of you.

If you or someone you know has been sexually abused, then please stand up. Be brave enough to stop the cycle. Bill was a monster, but my mum and my Nanna also failed to protect me by not standing up, that makes them complicit. Those secrets hurt people.

Talking about the abuse I suffered has helped me to put it behind me. I've told my story to encourage others to do the same and to stop these secrets and to remind us that there is no shame.

We Are Strong!

I've written a lot in these pages about my experiences in the police service and some of them are pretty horrific. I hold no grudges against the QPS, it was a different time and a different way. The stark reality is that if I hadn't had my own childhood trauma then I may have coped much better with the things that I faced.

Regardless of that. I survived and now I'm thriving. I found that I could go on and I could change my life. That's the message I want you to take from this. No matter how bad it gets, no matter how down you feel, find that curiosity, that hope, that next step and you will find your way. AND don't do it on your own. Call a friend, call a helpline – call me. Understand that there are people, maybe people who are strangers to you now, who you can lean on when the way gets tough.

Because we're all stronger together.

You CAN do it!

While writing this and reliving these moments I have cried. I can't forget those moments, they will always be a part of me. However, as much as they hurt, I accept them. They happened, I can't change that. I have chosen to face them, to swallow them as part of the tapestry that is my life and to value the lessons that I have learned from them.

Therefore, I've chosen to be happy. I've chosen to squeeze happiness out of the everyday. Even the boring days. Especially the boring days.

Imagine if your last breath on earth was after a boring day in the office. Would you regret it?

Now I try to make the boring days less boring. I try to have fun.

And here's the thing. I'm not talking about trying to make each day a grand adventure. I'm not asking you to go skydiving or anything extreme. I'm asking you to let the kid in you out of that overcoat you're wearing. Don't take the everyday for granted.

Get outside. Sit under a tree. Go a different way to work. Put some music on while you do the housework. Get up from your desk and move around. Don't be afraid of the rain. Go outside and get soaked. Stand barefoot on the grass and squelch your toes in the mud.

Find the things that you like doing and do more of them.

Remember!

You will make more shit decisions in your life. When you do, own them, learn from them and move on. Sometimes others will do bad shit to you. Recover from it, learn from it and move on. Random bad shit may happen to you. You'll get knocked down when it happens. Just keep on getting back up.

You get to choose.

Be brave enough to change when you have to.

Be brave enough to love.

Be brave enough to leave behind those who stop you from moving forward.

Be brave enough to let others know when you need help.

Most of all, be brave enough to be you.

Because you're you. There's no-one else on the planet like you, so make every day that you have here count.

The End

www.ingramcontent.com/pod-product-compliance
Lightning Source LLC
Chambersburg PA
CBHW041257040426
42334CB00028BA/3054